Hong Kong

Footprint

Emma Levine

Contents

Listings

About the author

Emma Levine first caught the Asia bug (but not SARS) in 1992 when exploring the continent armed with a camera and a thirst for adventure. She fell in love with Hong Kong a few months later, based herself on Lantau for four years and published her first books on Asian cricket. She worked and travelled widely throughout Asia, including China, Pakistan, Iran and Kyrgyzstan. She then shifted base to Mumbai, then Istanbul, and continued writing, photographing, and learning everything about Indian food and Turkish football. In London, she wrote and presented a documentary series about weird Asian sports, and still jets off to Asia whenever possible, especially to Istanbul, her second home.

Acknowledgements

Huge thanks in Hong Kong go to Ian Savage for his great knowledge and company whilst traipsing round the territory's lesser-known sights; Karen Swindall for giving me hospitality (in my old flat!); my other great friends Anne, Stuart and 'our Jack' Hellier for putting up with me and sending last-minute information and to the returnee Steve Langley who found time in the pressures of work to help me out. In Macau, a huge thank you to Teresa Gomes from the Macau Government Tourist Office for giving me a fabulous guided tour in style.

This book is dedicated to the memory of Louise Wolffe.

Gleaming glass towers, ceaseless choices of shopping and eating, tacky modern-day icons like Hello Kitty and fast food, the old double-decker trams and Star Ferry, and a full on pulsating energy that will invigorate the most hardened globetrotter – Hong Kong is all that plus deserted beaches, traditional fishing villages and the country parks covering more than two-thirds of the territory. The sight of Victoria harbour lit up at night is almost worth a 12-hour flight in itself, the delight enhanced by experiencing it at different times and from different places. Hong Kong is driven by its energy to work hard and play hard; long hours in the office are compensated for by a vibrant nightlife, variety of cuisine and swanky bars, – the 'in' places fluctuating as much as its Stock Exchange. Its greatest appeal lies in its diversity: the congested markets of Mongkok and the shopping streets of Wan Chai and Causeway Bay seem worlds away from the decadence of the Peak, location of some of the world's richest homes and the extreme wealth that Hong Kong's unwavering spirit of capitalism has allowed to flourish.

Spiritual and traditional

Despite the obvious love of shopping and eating, the perpetually crowded streets, glitzy neon lights and hard-core work ethic, it can all be put into context when you consider that the most expensive houses and powerful banks could not be planned without close consultation with the feng shui master. Look at the elegant sharp angles of the Bank of China building, or the high-tech iconic HSBC in Central, then realize that their exact location was plotted with due consideration to keeping the spirits and dragons happy. Somehow this spiritual side of Hong Kong neutralizes some of its commercial excesses and is a great leveller. Even stepping inside any temple a few feet away from a traffic jam reveals the respect that many Chinese people always have for their religious and cultural traditions, whether burning paper money for loved ones to enjoy "on the other side" or eating mooncakes to celebrate mid-Autumn festival.

Rural escapes

But away from the noisy bars, crowds clogging Causeway Bay, obsession with share prices and those dragging shopping trolleys in Mongkok markets, few people would associate Hong Kong with deserted beaches, wild walks over the hills, bird sanctuaries and dolphin watching. Most visitors only experience, and usually love, the excesses of noise, lights and action of urban life and understand the "city that never sleeps" cliché. But more than two-thirds of the territory – made up of Hong Kong Island, Kowloon, New Territories and outlying islands – consists of country parks. Hop over the water to Lantau to see the huge bronze Buddha, the last surviving fishing village with aluminium stilt houses, the challenging Lantau Peak trek or take a boat trip to spot pink dolphins. The traditional walled villages in the New Territories reveal Hong Kong's history of clan structure, while wandering around Sai Kung's vast expanse of hills and reservoirs will make you forget that just the previous day you were haggling for clothes in Tsim Sha Tsui.

At a glance

Hong Kong Island

The business and shopping district of **Central** is a great place to get your first (and last) impression of Hong Kong, with its shiny skyscrapers, narrow street markets, Star Ferry and international cuisine. **Sheung Wan** is very traditionally Chinese, with the Macau Ferry Terminal, Western Market and Sheung Wan Gala Point and its wholesale trade in Chinese medicine. East of Central is **Wan Chai**, rather sleazy in the old days and now great entertainment, especially the bars of Lockhart Road and thrift-shopper's heaven Hennessy Road. **Causeway Bay** is intense consumerism: always crowded and polluted, with chic Japanese department stores opposite cramped stalls selling plastic watches. **Happy Valley** is dominated by the racecourse which every Wednesday night sees millions of dollars spent (and usually lost). Towards the northeast of the island is **North Point**, less upmarket commercial and more traditional, with Marble Street market and a couple of interesting museums and temples around **Shau Kai Wan** and **Sai Wan Ho**, including the new Hong Kong Film Archives. A ride up to **The Peak**, preferably on the historic Peak Tram, reveals the best harbour views and some of the world's most valuable property. Villages around the **south of Hong Kong Island** range from the traditional fishing village of **Aberdeen** with junk boats bobbing around the harbour, to the holiday-friendly **Stanley**, famous for its market. **Ocean Park** is a favourite with kids with plenty to occupy a full day. **Shek O** is a wealthy expat enclave with a dramatic setting via a breathtaking bus ride and **Repulse Bay** has one of the best beaches in Hong Kong, packed at weekends.

Kowloon

Kowloon peninsula is not as glamorous as Central, but has some great sights and very traditional Chinese areas. **Tsim Sha Tsui** represents Hong Kong's shameless commercialism at its very, er, best and it takes a strong stamina to conquer crowded Golden Mile on foot. The walkway by the Cultural Centre offers a wonderful harbour view and every morning sees the calming tai chi sessions. North along Nathan Road is **Kowloon Park**, a swathe of green, complete with outdoor swimming pools and an aviary. Further north, the streets between **Jordan** and **Yau Ma Tei** reveal Chinese culture in all its glory, laden with street markets selling live snakes, frogs and chickens. Temple Street Night Market is the place to haggle for souvenirs, experience amateur traditional Cantonese Opera and even get your palm read. **Mongkok**, typically Chinese, is one of the world's most densely populated areas but you can escape the crowds in the Bird Garden where old men take their caged birds for walks. Eastern Kowloon's **Diamond Hill** and **Wong Tai Sin** are uninspiring residential areas but worth visiting for the graceful Chi Lin Nunnery and the Wong Tai Sin Temple.

New Territories

This northernmost area of the territory between Kowloon and the Chinese border has witnessed radical development of parts of its rugged coastline, mountains and vast green expanse, although there is still a sizeable area of country parks and traditional walled villages. **Sha Tin** is one of its biggest towns and, although not pretty, has a couple of great attractions including the Museum of Heritage, one of Hong Kong's best. Sha Tin racecourse buzzes at weekends and the nearby Ten Thousand Buddhas Monastery is worth trekking up the 400 steps to. Further north is the Chinese University with a wonderful art museum that plays an important role in promoting Chinese art and further north still is **Tai Po**, one of the oldest-known settlements in Hong Kong. A short cab ride away, Kadoorie Farm and Botanical Garden is a huge hilltop farm with walking trails, animal conservatories, exotic plants and animals. Ornithologists will love **Mai Po Marshes** on the northwestern border. In the eastern New Territories, **Sai Kung** is a fishing village and popular expat enclave, and a good base for hiking around the surrounding acres of country parks and isolated beaches, especially over to **Plover Cove**.

Outlying Islands

Lantau is the largest of the Outlying Islands and twice the size of Hong Kong Island, with small villages dotted around its open spaces. As home to the airport, transport to and from Lantau has substantially improved since 1999. The immense Big Buddha sees daily busloads of visitors, thankfully less to the peaceful, traditional fishing village of Tai O. Cheung Sha beach is one of Hong Kong's best and blissfully quiet during the week. **Lamma** has had a longstanding reputation as a hippie haven and, although its main village is like a badly designed holiday resort, it has some lovely short walks, a couple of decent beaches and good restaurants. Lively **Cheung Chau** is tiny, yet the most densely populated island, with a string of great seafood restaurants along the waterfront and is famous for its huge Bun Festival. **Peng Chau** is even smaller and worth a walk around for its relatively undisturbed island life and the picturesque **Po Toi Islands** are some of the most remote and unspoilt areas of Hong Kong.

Macau

A Portuguese colony until 1999, now reverted to Chinese rule, Macau is a favourite weekend getaway for Hong Kongers who take advantage of its legal casinos. With a relaxed ambience, Macau's beauty lies in discovering its churches, fortresses, temples and cobbled squares, plus the Mediterranean flavour of its architecture. And, of course, the Macanese cuisine and love of long lunches washed down with Portuguese wine is a hugely enjoyable part of the experience. Away from the main peninsula, part of the China mainland, are two islands in the Pearl River Delta: **Taipa** has restored elegant mansions, old shophouses, a Sunday market and a whole host of good local restaurants; while **Coloane** has a couple of beaches and country parks good for trekking.

Best

Ten of the best

1 **The Peak** Sip a cocktail at sunset and soak up one of the greatest views in the world: the Hong Kong skyline, p60.

2 **Temple Street** After haggling for goodies in the Night Market, hum along to some backstreet Cantonese Opera and drink a bowl of snake soup, p75.

3 **Wong Tai Sin Temple** Brave the thick clouds of incense smoke at one of the largest temples in the territory, then have your fortune sticks read by one of 160 soothsayers, p80.

4 **Cheung Chau** Choose your own seafood swimming in tanks outside the restaurants, then feast on the freshly cooked delights while gazing at the sea, p104.

5 **Cat Street** Haggle for an antique birdcage or Mao memorabilia while trying to distinguish between antiques and junk, p48.

6 **Tai O** Take a sampan trip around the few remaining stilt houses in this old Lantau village, once a den of piracy, p98.

7 **Macau** Go greyhound racing at Asia's only dog track, and have your photograph taken with ex-champion Cheeky Cat, p111.

8 **Tram ride** Take the top deck from Kennedy Town to North Point, and look down on the crowds without being trampled by them, p30.

9 **Tai Chi** Learn the centuries-old martial art, with an early morning lesson with the experts at Star Ferry Pier in Tsim Sha Tsui, p33.

10 **Sai Kung** Burn off the calories from all that feasting on Chinese food with an exhilarating hike around the territories' vast country parks, p83.

The ★ symbol is used throughout this guide to indicate recommended sights.

Trip planner

Hong Kong has a subtropical climate with significant seasonal changes: spring is warm and humid, averaging in the 70's but cooler in the evenings. Summer can be unbearably hot, reaching 90° and a sweaty 90% humidity, which many try to avoid. The clear, sunny days of autumn, usually in the 70's, are the most comfortable. Winter is the coldest and driest season with chilly evenings, and extra layers required if venturing to the higher altitudes, outlying islands or New Territories. Autumn and spring are the most popular tourist seasons, and around Chinese New Year (January/February) and Christmas are the busiest times to fly.

May to November is typhoon season, although they usually occur during summer. The intense winds can, at worst, cause great destruction to buildings and lives, although this is rare and the damage is usually limited to ferries being cancelled.

24 hours

After a dim sum breakfast at **Luk Yu Tea House**, ascend the mid-levels escalator to **Hollywood Road**'s antique shops, **Cat Street** and **Man Mo Temple**. Return to Central and take the bus or Peak Tram to **The Peak**. After a walk, cocktail or dinner, take the MTR to **Temple Street Night Market** to enjoy cheap goodies, backstreet Cantonese Opera and fortune-tellers. The **Star Ferry** back to Central has that million-dollar harbour view and, if you have stamina, hit **SoHo**'s bars and clubs till dawn.

A long weekend

If you have an extra couple of days in the city, add to the above with day on **Lantau**, starting with a climb up the **Big Buddha** followed by a vegetarian lunch at the monastery. Take the bus or taxi to **Tai O** and explore the old fishing village, then end the day on **Cheung Sha beach** and dine while gazing at the sea.

Start the next morning with a **tai chi lesson** by Tsim Sha Tsui's

Cultural Centre, then visit the Hong Kong Story exhibition in the **Museum of History**. Walk up **Nathan Road**'s Golden Mile and swim in the outdoor pool in **Kowloon Park**. Meander between Yuen Po Street Bird Garden, the Flower and Goldfish Markets in **Mongkok**, then have tea in Peninsula Hotel – or brave the grubby **Chungking Mansions** for a cheap (and tasty) Indian meal.

Alternatively, take a walk around **Central**'s architectural stunners, then through the Chinese medicine trading areas of **Sheung Wan**. Board the top deck of a tram to **Causeway Bay** and, if it's a Wednesday, have a flutter at **Happy Valley Racecourse**.

A week

Spend three-four days in the thick of the city to experience shopping, cultural and architectural delights of Central, Sheung Wan, Tsim Sha Tsui and Mongkok, contrasted with a more peaceful day to an outlying island like Lantau (see above).

Then spend a day in **eastern Kowloon**, visiting the graceful Chi Lin Nunnery, and nearby Wong Tai Sin Temple. Head north into the New Territories, to the **Museum of Heritage** in Sha Tin, and make the steep climb to the **Ten Thousand Buddhas Monastery**.

If you like walking, spend a day in the New Territories' **country parks**, starting in the fishing village of **Sai Kung**. Explore some of the 7500 hectares of open countryside and finish up by choosing your own fresh fish in the waterfront restaurants.

A couple of days in **Macau** will probably involve exploring the Leal Senado, Ruinas Sao Paulo and its quaint antique shops. Take the world's shortest cable-car journey to Gaia Fort and Lighthouse and wander round the Old Protestant cemetery and Casa Garden. Indulge in a traditional Chinese tea-making ceremony at the Culture Club, visit A-Ma temple and then take a Chinese junk tour. Taipa village merits at least half a day with its old village shophouses and Mediterranean-style courtyards. Spend a night out at the Canindrome, Asia's only greyhound track, and of course every trip to Macau should involve a leisurely sampling of Macanese cuisine.

Contemporary Hong Kong

It's hard to believe that 150 years ago Hong Kong was described as 'that barren rock' when today it has become a world-famous trading and business centre. Refugees from China during the 20th century laid the groundwork for its successful manufacturing industry and strong work ethic and this is still an integral part of contemporary life. People work hard and play hard and parents put great pressure on their kids to achieve academic success.

The usually strong economy has suffered severe dents over the last few years: uncertainty surrounding the 1997 handover, a severe Asian recession in 1998, tourists keeping their distance post-September 11 and then the 2003 SARS virus causing many small businesses to close and unemployment to rise to around 5%. But Hong Kong people are resiliant, and even when SARS was at its worst, they showed their innate need to dress up, spend and enjoy – fake designer masks gracing many faces.

The years of being one of the world's greatest business centres, combined with the Chinese love of money and gambling have, not surprisingly, filtered into everyday life and culture. From the plethora of high-tech banks and besuited briefcase-carrying brokers, to the obsession with fashion labels and being seen in the swankiest restaurants, spending money is everyone's favourite sport. (And if Gucci or Prada are beyond your means, a decent fake will do nearly as well.) But that's not to say that everyone has money to burn. Although the Peak and Repulse Bay allow a glimpse of some of the world's most expensive property, most people live in tiny rented apartments in public housing blocks (possibly explaining why entire families make late-night shopping and dining trips). Responding to social unrest, slums and the need to house Chinese immigrants post-Cultural Revolution, the Government built these blocks in the 1960s. Land reclamation and 'new towns' in the New Territories also helped to house a massive population in a relatively tiny area.

But, although clusters of grey concrete blocks are never far away,

Hong Kong is famous for its groundbreaking architectural wonders, like the high-tech glam of the Hongkong Shanghai Bank and the Bank of China. These monuments in glass and steel are a means of propaganda – a great statement declaring the territory's prosperity and success to the world. A more recent phenomenon is its post-modernist architecture, more subtle creations using marble and granite. Exchange Square in Central is a superb example.

When Hong Kong reverted to Chinese rule on 1 July 1997, the territory bade farewell to British Governor Chris Patten and said hello to Chief Executive Tung Chee-hwa. The world then watched anxiously to see if the entrepreneurial spirit and relatively liberal society would be radically altered. Most visitors will experience the same surface characteristics of Hong Kong; the energy, consumerism and attractions that existed pre-97. Little has changed regarding economic structure and business, which works as 'one country, two systems' and retains a high degree of autonomy. Most issues are dealt with from Hong Kong and only matters concerning defence and international politics are dictated by Beijing.

However, since the end of 2002, concern increased surrounding the prospect of Article 23 being incorporated into the constitution, thus outlawing treason, secession, sedition and subversion. In China, guilt can be implied simply by expressing political dissent, leading to heavy prison sentences, so it's easy to understand why people fear the erosion of free speech and human rights. Since the Tiananmen Square massacre in 1989, worries have arisen about the political might of Beijing and the prospect of the People's Liberation Army patrolling Hong Kong's streets. Over a million people in Hong Kong demonstrated against Tiananmen, and there is an annual candlelit vigil on each anniversary. But, since 1997, organizers of demonstrations of more than 29 people need a permit at least 48 hours in advance. This didn't prevent huge protests against Article 23, however, including an incredible one million people marching on 1st July 2003. In the face of such massive public opposition, plus the resignation of the Secretary of

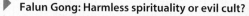

▶ Falun Gong: Harmless spirituality or evil cult?

Followers of Falun Gong say their philosophy, slow-motion exercise and meditation, promote good health and moral living, within the core teaching of truth, compassion and tolerance. However, the Chinese Government is worried about the group's ability to organize itself, reckoning it to be an evil cult controlled by its US-based founder who spreads superstition and malicious fallacies. Because of this suspicion, the Government outlawed and persecuted Falun Gong members in 1999, scared by their sheer numbers and growing visibility since its beginnings in the early 1990s. The matter came to a head in April 1999 when 10,000 followers showed up at the Communist Party HQ in Beijing, clad in their yellow t-shirts, to demonstrate for official recognition. Since being banned and outlawed, there have been increasing reports of persecution, unlawful imprisonment and torture.

So how does this affect Hong Kong? There are thousands of followers in the SAR and until now have been assured that they face no problems, even though many claim that they are 'under watch' and that Hong Kong regularly refuses entry to US Falun Gong believers. There was a serious and growing worry about Article 23, but now that has been put on hold, at least they can sleep in peace – for a while anyway.

Security Regina Yip, Tung Chee-hwa had little choice but to reopen consultation and eventually, on September 5th 2003, withdrew the act indefinitely.

Despite being under British rule for 150 years and a business centre attracting foreign expatriate workers, Hong Kong's population, culture and language is essentially Cantonese. People of predominantly Chinese descent make up 95% of the population; the

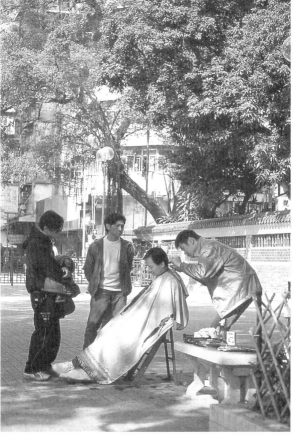

Short back and sides
The public square at Tin Hau Temple on Temple Street is as good a place as any for a Hong Kong haircut.

largest groups of foreign nationals are from the Philippines and Indonesia, mainly working as domestic servants; and from Canada and the USA. Although English was the official language along with Cantonese, the number of people speaking it has declined since 1997. Putonghua, referred to in the West as Mandarin, is the preferred second language and is now part of the school curriculum.

Hong Kong Chinese have always been relatively tolerant towards other religions, probably because their own Buddhist, Taoist and Confuciunist worshippers often share the same temple, but there is not always an easy mix of Chinese with other nationalities. European and western foreigners are often referred to as *gweilo*, translating rather unflatteringly as 'foreign/white devil'; and black people and those from the subcontinent are often seen as inferior.

Contemporary youth culture is largely imported and can appear, from a Westerner's perspective, as highly childlike: small plastic toys hanging from the most sophisticated designer handbag, the love of the Japanese icon Hello Kitty, and the adoration of English slapstick comedy like Mr Bean. Cantopop, that most indigenous of music genres, mixes sugary naïvety with the well-groomed finesse of its male and female stars, essentially formulaic in their looks and products. There is precious little radical fashion, music or opinion, possibly because self-expression and independent thought is rarely encouraged. But one benefit of a relatively well-behaved society is an extremely low crime rate with vandalism and graffiti (however, see p71) practically non-existent. Family life is important and while there is great respect for older people, young children are patently cherished.

Getting to Hong Kong usually means a long-haul flight with one of the many airlines flying from England, America, Canada and Australia, some of them non-stop and some with one or two connections. Many people use Hong Kong as a stopover between, for example, London and Australia, but if Hong Kong is your final destination it may be possible to add another city into the journey at no extra cost. Air fares rocket around August and tickets are more expensive and hard to come by around Christmas and Chinese New Year (Jan/Feb). From China, it's now an easy journey over the Lo Wu border by train, and there's a decent bus service from Guanzhou, plus catamarans and ferries from south China and Macau.

Hong Kong's public transport network is one of the best in the world with fast, comfortable and cheap buses, underground (MTR), minibuses and ferries, plus plenty of taxis. In the New Territories, the KCR (Kowloon-Canton Railway) goes as far as the Chinese border. As most buses only accept exact change, an Octopus card is the best option, a rechargeable ticket which can be used on nearly all transport.

Getting there

Hong Kong is a genuine 24-hour city and extremely safe, so a late-night arrival is never a problem, although most flights land 0600-2400. The airport's hotel booking office (see p119) is open within these hours should you arrive with no reservation and pitching up at a hotel at any time of night is fine. The airport express train runs into the city between 0550 and 0115; bus 0600-2400; MTR 0600-2300; and there taxis through the night. Once in the city, there will always be somewhere open for food or a beer even at dawn, ranging from convenience stores to hotel cafés. Hung Hom train station is equally safe with all-night transport available and the Macau Ferry terminal has taxis round the clock long after the MTR and buses have finished.

Air

From Europe There are daily, non-stop flights between London and Hong Kong, taking around 12 hours with **Cathay Pacific**, **Virgin** and **British Airways**. In addition, most major European airlines fly non-stop from their respective major cities, for example **Air France** from Paris, **Lufthansa** from Frankfurt and **KLM** from Amsterdam and a ticket from London will often be cheaper with a connection at one of these places. **Gulf Air** and **Emirates** can also be cheap. From Europe, prices vary quite widely from month to month, the most expensive times are in August and just before and after Christmas, but even then, booking well in advance, you can get tickets from around £600. Book too late, and you may be stumped with a £1500 fare. The cheapest months are around May and November with prices coming down by around 50%.

From North America From New York, Montreal and many other North American cities, flights have one or two stops and the journey takes around 20 hours. From Montreal, there are several airlines operating daily flights, including **United Airlines**, **Air Canada** and **Continental**, usually touching down in Chicago or

→ **Airlines and travel agents**

Australia Qantas Airlines (holidays telephone line) T 131415, www.qantas.com; **Cathay Pacific** T 131747, www.cathaypacific.com/au; **Travel Supermarket** (packages, flights and insurance) T 132243; **Trailfinder** (cheap flights) T (02) 9247 7666 (Sydney), (03) 9600 3022 (Melbourne), (08) 9226 1222 (Perth), www.trailfinders.com.au; **Travelscene** (flights and packages) T 131398; **Flight Centre** (flights and packages) T 131600.

Canada Air Canada T 1888 247 2262, www.aircanada.ca

Ireland Trailfinders (cheap flights) T (01) 677 7888 (Dublin), www.trailfinders.ie

New Zealand Kasbah www.kasbah.com; **Air New Zealand** T 0800 247 764, www.airnz.co.nz

United Kingdom Virgin Atlantic T 01293 450 150, www.virgin-atlantic.com; **British Airways** T 0845 773 3377, www.ba.com; **Cathay Pacific** T 020 8834 8888, www.cathaypacific.com; **Trailfinders** T 020 7628 7628, www.trailfinders.co.uk; **STA Travel** T 08701 600599, www.statravel.com; **Dial-A-Flight** T 7369 1885, www.dialaflight.com

USA Continental Airlines T 1800 525 0280, www.continental.com; **Virgin Atlantic** T 1800 862 8621, www.virgin-atlantic.com; **American Airlines** T 18 433 7300, www.aa.com

Other websites
www.expedia.com
www.travelocity.com
www.ebookers.com
www.opodo.com
www.cheapflights.com

Boston and prices range from around US$1,000 (May) to US$2,000 (December). From New York the journey time is around the same, although prices are lower, from US$700 to US$1,200.

From Australia/New Zealand Frequent flights with **Qantas** and **Cathay Pacific**, many of which are non-stop, go daily from Melbourne, Sydney and other Australian cities, with prices around the A$1,000 mark, journey time 8-10 hours. From Auckland, these airlines, plus **Air New Zealand**, fly non-stop (11 hours) or via Melbourne, Sydney or Brisbane. Prices are around A$1,200 in April, and A$1,500 in August, although the high and low seasons tend not to be as noticeable as from other destinations.

Airport information Gone are the days of the white-knuckle landing into Kowloon's Kai Tak Airport: **Chep Lap Kok** on Lantau (airport information www.hkairport.com, flight information **T** 2181 0000) is one of the world's largest, most expensive and best equipped airports. It contains a good collection of duty-free and designer shops, restaurants, bars, a beauty salon, children's entertainment area, showers and business centre. There's a tourist counter in Arrivals with maps and leaflets. Once outside, staff at the excellent transport information counter will explain the various options for getting into the city, which include the high-speed **Airport Express** rail service (see page 30), a plethora of bus routes including the **Airbus** (buses running from the airport, which leave every 10-15 minutes, include: A11, North Point Ferry Pier, via Central, HK$40; A21, Hung Hom KCR, via Tsim Sha Tsui, HK$33; A35, Mui Wo, HK$14, Sundays and pub hols HK$23), and a large taxi rank (expect to pay around HK$300 to get to Central). Most public transport operates between around 0600-0100. There are ATM machines, banks and left-luggage in Arrivals.

   Hong Kong Hotels Association booking counter is in Buffer Halls A and B, **T** 2383 8380 (Hall A), **T** 2769 8822 (Hall B), 0600-2400. www.hkta.org/hkha, hkhahrc@att.net.hk

→ Travel extras

Safety Both Hong Kong and Macau are among the safest cities in the world. Walking around, using public transport late at night and leaving nightclubs at 0300 is safe even for lone women and personal attacks or muggings are almost unheard of. However, like anywhere in the world, pickpockets do exist so take care of wallets and other valuables while in crowded places, and don't leave bags unattended. Over the border into China, however, is a different story and extreme care should be taken of bag snatchers and pickpockets, who are often young children.

Money and tipping The Hong Kong dollar is loosely pegged to the US dollar at around 1US\$ = HK\$7.8. The Macau Pataca (MOP) is worth almost exactly that of the Hong Kong dollar. But while dollars are used in Macau, patacas are no use outside, so it is easier to stick to dollars. Both currencies may be withdrawn from Macau ATMs.

Most hotels and restaurants add 10% to the bill, so an extra tip is not required and when service charge has not been added, an approximate 10% tip is appreciated. Small tips may also be given to porters in smart hotels. Some trendy bars try the American method of handing change on a plate, but this is to the customer's discretion. For taxi fares, rounding up to the nearest dollar is the norm.

Vaccinations The standard of health and hygiene is generally pretty good, although eating fish caught in Hong Kong waters has previously been known to spread hepatitis A. The following vaccinations are recommended (more strongly recommended if travelling here frequently or for a long period): Typhoid, hepatitis A and B, diptheria and TB. Contact your doctor up to 3 months before travelling and for up-to-date advice.

Visas Most nationalities are given a free 90-day visa on arrival including most Europeans, and those from Canada, USA, Australia and New Zealand. British citizens get 180 days.

Getting around

Hong Kong's public transport is among the best in the world and makes getting around the city very easy. If you're staying for more than a couple of days, it's well worth paying a $100 deposit for an **Octopus**, an electronic top-up card which is swiped and deducted on the MTR, bus, tram and most ferries and can even be used in the 7-11 store. They can be topped up at MTR stations and the deposit and excess payment refunded from here also. The journeys are slightly cheaper, but more importantly it avoids the inconvenience of having to produce the exact change.

Bus

Double- and single-decker buses cover most of the territory with destinations marked in English and Chinese, although drivers usually speak little English. Most buses run from 0600-2400, with a few night services, indicated by 'N' prefixing the service number. The exact fare is required on boarding (coins or Octopus card), the price is displayed next to the driver and ranges from around $1.50 (short hop) to $40 (a huge area). Air-conditioned buses cost a little more. Timetables are written in English at all bus stops. Many larger MTR stations outside the centre have an adjacent bus station. Both buses and roads get congested during rush hours. Hong Kong Island buses are operated by **New World First Bus Co**, **T** 2136 8888; and **Citybus T** 2873 1818 (also in Kowloon and New Territories); Kowloon buses by **Kowloon Motor Bus Co**, **T** 2745 4466.

From **Central Bus Terminal** (Exchange Square) buses 6, 6A and 260 go to Stanley via Deep Water Bay and Repulse Bay; 15 to The Peak; 70 for Aberdeen and 90 to Ocean Park. From **Outlying Islands Ferry Piers Bus Terminal** buses 11 and 681 go to Causeway Bay via Admiralty. From **Tsim Sha Tsui, Star Ferry Terminal** buses 1, 1A, 2, 6, 6A, 7 and 9 go to Temple Street Night Market via Kowloon Park. Other useful routes include: 5A between Kennedy Town to Happy Valley, via Admiralty, Central and Wan Chai;

2 between Macau Ferry Terminal and Shau Kei Wan via Wan Chai and Causeway Bay; 91 between Diamond Hill MTR and Sai Kung, via Clearwater Bay; and 9 between Shau Kei Wan MTR and Shek O.

Minibuses (Public Light Bus) Often operating in areas where there is no MTR, these are faster than buses and all carry 14-16 people. Destinations are written on signboards on the front, but not always in English, so ask before boarding. Maxicabs (cream vans with red stripe), do not have fixed stops and will pick up and drop off where requested, pay the driver on exit (will give change). Minibuses (cream with green stripe) operate with fixed routes and stops, payment on boarding. Some accept Octopus cards.

To China Numerous public and private bus companies travel between Hong Kong and Shenzhen leaving every 15 minutes from different parts of Hong Kong but mainly stopping at Kowloon Tong and Hung Hom. **China Travel Service**, 78 Connaught Rd, Central, **T** 2853 3534, www.chinats.com, can organize tickets and visas.

Car
There must be a reason why most cars on the road in the city are either being chauffeur-driven or are taxis. There seems little sense in driving, with traffic snarls throughout the day, so hiring a car seems completely pointless given the quality and choice of public transport and taxis.

Cycling
Forget cycling anywhere in the city: the traffic is too intense to make it pleasurable or safe and walking is a more enjoyable option and of course public transport is widespread and cheap. That said, Lantau, Lamma, Cheung Chau, Shek O and other rural areas have bikes for hire which is far more enjoyable, costing around $30-40/day, perhaps a little more at weekends. See Mountain biking, p206.

Ferry

Star Ferry The most famous of Hong Kong's ferries, this shuttle service taking between 8 and 15 minutes runs between Central and Wan Chai to Tsim Sha Tsui and Hung Hom. Enquiries **T** 2366 2576, www.starferry.com.hk (see p37.) **Central-Hung Hom** and **Wan Chai-Hung Hom**; Mon-Sat 0700-1900, every 15-20 mins. $5.30, $2.70 children. **Wan Chai-Tsim Sha Tsui**, 0730-2300, every 8-20 mins. $2.20, $1.30 children. **Central-Tsim Sha Tsui**; 0630-2330, every 4-10 mins. $2.20, $1.30 children.

To Outlying Islands Most ferries to the outlying islands of Lantau, Lamma, Cheung Chau and Peng Chau leave from the Central Ferry Pier, west of Star Ferry pier. Timetables are posted at each pier entrance next to the ticket booths. If travelling on Sunday or public holidays, be prepared for crowded and noisy journeys (buy a return ticket to save queuing on the way back). Most ferries have a small open deck at the back, making evening departure or arrival into Central more like a luxury cruise. Prices rise on Sundays and public holidays, for fast ferries, and on the air-conditioned upper deck of the slow ferries. **New World First Ferry**, **T** 2131 8181, www.nwff.com.hk, operates services to Mui Wo, Cheung Chau and Peng Chau. **Hong Kong and Kowloon Ferry**, **T** 2815 6063, operates the Lamma ferry. All the following times are approximate.

Central-Mui Wo (Lantau): 0600-2400 approx every 20 mins. 0100-0600 approx every 2-3 hours. **Central-Yung Shue Wan (Lamma)**: 0630-0030 approx every 20-60 mins. **Aberdeen-Yung Shue Wan**: 0600-2100 approx every 60 mins. **Central-Sok Kwu Wan**: 0700-2300 approx every 90 mins. **Central-Peng Chau**: 0700-2330 approx every 60 mins, 0030-0700 approx every 3 hours. **Central-Discovery Bay**: 0620-2400 approx every 10-20 mins, 2400-0600 approx every 30-90 mins.

To Macau Catamarans and ferries for Macau now run through the night and approx every 15-30 minutes during the day, slowing to

→ Island Hopping Pass

If you can happily spend a day hopping on and off boats, **New World First Ferry Company** offers a day pass for $30 for unlimited travel on any ferries between Cheung Chau, Lantau and Peng Chau. A surcharge is payable in deluxe class, fast ferries, on Sundays and public holidays. The pass can be bought at the Central Outlying Ferry Pier or HKTB Visitors' Centres, T 2131 8181, ferry_ideas@nwff.com.hk, www.nwff.com.hk

every 2 hours after midnight. Book ahead – especially over weekends and holidays – and if returning late on Sunday night. (If you have no reserved seat you must queue as a standby passenger to see if there are available spaces.) The journey costs $131 weekdays, $141 weekends and $161 for the night service, both on the TurboJet leaving from Macau Ferry Terminal (Sheung Wan, 1 hour) and on the ferry from China Ferry Terminal (Tsim Sha Tsui, 60-75 minutes).

To China Between **China Ferry Terminal** and Shenzhen there are 6-8 catamarans daily, 0730-1800, $189 single. From **Macau Ferry Terminal** there is 1 at 0800 and 3 daily in the opposite direction, run by TurboJet. From **Kowloon** to Guanzhou there are 2 daily, costing around $198 single. There are many other Chinese cities served around the Pearl River Delta, including 7 daily to Zhuhai 0730-2130. **Turbojet**, T 2859 3333, www.Turbojet.com.hk **Macau Ferry Terminal**, T 2858 0909, 2526 5305. **China Ferry Terminal**, T 2730 3213, 2736 1387. Check in advance if you can get a visa on arrival.

Kaidos and sampans In addition to the regular services, smaller motor boats, usually operated by persuasive women, can or will take you anywhere you want, at a price. These can be a good way of getting back to one of the Outlying Islands, for example from

Aberdeen to Lamma, after the last ferries have gone. Tung Lung is accessible by keido on weekends and public holidays, **T** 2560 9929.

Taxi

Plentiful, reliable and cheap, taxis ply most areas of Hong Kong. Hong Kong Island and Kowloon taxis are red, with a flag-fall of $15 and $1.40 for every subsequent 200m. Those in the New Territories are green, Lantau are blue, and both are a little cheaper. If taking a cab between Kowloon and Hong Kong Island you may be charged double the tunnel fee to pay for the car to return again. Cabbies are very good at putting on the meter and usually pretty honest but not many speak English so have your destination written in Chinese.

Lantau has the worst taxi system in Hong Kong and painfully too few vehicles given the amount of visitors at weekends. If you are requiring a taxi from Lantau to the airport, the company try to charge an extra $70 for making an advance booking of more than 1 hour. If it is a Sunday or public holiday it may be better to get the airport bus, which is almost as quick.

Train

Mass Transit Railway (MTR) The MTR is the fastest and easiest way to cover long journeys and it is a pure delight to experience an underground system that is clean, efficient and safe. Most lines operate between 0600-0100 daily. They are slightly less regular on major public holidays and every station has its first and last train clearly displayed. Typical single fares include $4 for a couple of stops, $7.50 crossing the entire Island line and $13 from Central to Tsuen Wan (half price for children and senior citizens). There are four lines which cover nearly all the urban areas: **Island line** runs from Sheung Wan to Chai Wan; **Tsuen Wan line** runs from Central across to Kowloon via Tsim Sha Tsui and Mongkok. **Kwun Tong line** connects Yau Ma Tei to Tiu Keng Leng via Kowloon Tong; and **Yseung Kwan O line** – North Point to Po Lam in Kowloon. **MTR Enquiries**: **T** 2881 8888, www.mtr.com.hk

Kowloon-Canton Railway (KCR) Running between Hung Hom in Tsim Sha Tsui East, this is the quickest route to the China border (open 0630-2400), taking around 40 minutes to Lo Wu on the Hong Kong side. This route is overground and passes through New Territory towns and villages like Sha Tin, Tai Po and Fanling via Mongkok and Kowloon Tong interchange. Trains run every 3-20 minutes 0530-0020. Single tickets to the border cost $33. Once reaching Lo Wu, the crossing into Shenzhen is easy and from the main railway station there are 40 high-speed trains a day to Guangzhou. Many nationalities can obtain a Chinese visa at the border, but check before leaving, and allow a couple of days for the visa if necessary. There are also 7 daily through trains from Hung Hom to Guanzhou. **KCR Enquiries**: **T** 2602 7799, www.kcrc.com **Hung Hom station**, **T** 2602 7799, www.kcrc.com, is in Tsim Sha Tsui East (also called the KCR station). It is accessible by a complex walkway and flyover and there is transport to and from it all night.

Airport Express Link The fast rail link between Hong Kong Station (Central) and the airport, via Kowloon Station, takes 23 minutes, costs $100 single, and runs between 0550-0048 from Hong Kong. Baggage may be checked in for flights with major airlines at both Hong Kong and Kowloon stations once the train ticket has been bought.

Tram Since 1904, **Hong Kong Tramways** has been trundling its double-decker trams across Hong Kong Island between Kennedy Town and Shau Kei Wan, one of the oldest remaining systems in the world. It's still one of the loveliest ways of seeing the streets, albeit at a slow pace, especially from the top deck front seats. There is a flat fare of $2 ($1 for children and senior citizens) payable in the box on alighting, or by using an Octopus card.

Even older than that is the **Peak Tram**, a funicular railway at around 45° that connects Central to the top of Victoria Peak, running daily from 0700-2400. (See p61.)

Walking

Given the potential levels of heat and humidity, not to mention rain, it is not always practical to walk long distances within the city. However, with a pleasant climate, wandering the streets is the best way to see Hong Kong providing you can deal with crowds. Concentrating on one area, for example Central, SoHo and Sheung Wan is straightforward enough. Similarly, exploring Wan Chai to Causeway Bay makes for an interesting walk. Kowloon is a little more difficult, although starting at the south end of Tsim Sha Tsui and heading north up Nathan Road as far as Mongkok will take at least a couple of hours.

Tours

The **Hong Kong Tourist Board (HKTB)** (see p33) organizes some wonderful tours, including self-guided walking tours, bus trips to the New Territories, a night at the races and harbour cruises. It also runs the Cultural Kaleidoscope Program (see below), which includes various differently themed free talks or tours given by experts in certain fields. In addition it can recommend private agents who organize tours around the territory. Other tour operators include: **Gray Line Tours**, Room 501, 5/F Cheong Hing Building, 72 Nathan Rd, Tsim Sha Tsui, **T** 2723 1808, www.grayline.com.hk **Splendid Tours and Travel**, 2/F Sheraton HK Hotel and Towers, 20 Nathan Rd, Tsim Sha Tsui, **T** 2316 2151, www.splendidtours.com **C&A Tours**, Room 802 Koon Fook Center, 9 Knutsford Terr, Tsim Sha Tsui, **T** 2369 1866, www.cnatours.com **President Tours & Travel Service**, 9/F Tung Fai Building, 27 Cameron Rd, Tsim Sha Tsui, **T** 2369 4808. **JT Tours**, Room 1005, Landwide Commercial Building, 118-120 Austin Rd, Tsim Sha Tsui, **T** 2735 3028. *See also Kids, p215.*

Walking tours

The HKTB's self-guided walking tours are an ideal way of finding out more whilst walking and sightseeing at your own pace, without the restrictions of a group or guide. Portable audio equipment, a map and leaflet may be borrowed for a day from HKTB visitors' centres for a returnable deposit of $500.

Hong Kong Island walking tour takes in modern and historical architectural sights like St John's Cathedral, Hongkong Shanghai Bank and Statue Square; Kowloon guides you on a walk from the Star Ferry Clock Tower, past the Peninsula Hotel and up Nathan Road; the New Territories tour takes in Chinese temples and the famous Lam Tsuen wishing trees.

Hong Kong Walks is a leaflet detailing eight walks including some on the Outlying Islands, the Peak and Mongkok markets.

Cultural Kaleidoscope programme

The 'Meet the People' itinerary has different free themed talks or tours every day, most lasting an hour or two, giving a good insight into local culture. Details may be subject to change, so confirm and register via the HKTB's Visitors' Hotline, **T** 2508 1234.

Cantonese Opera Appreciation Tour A guide through the Museum's Cantonese Opera Hall, giving a better understanding of the art. Entrance of Hong Kong Heritage Museum, 1 Man Lam Rd, Sha Tin. Sat, 1430-1545.

Chinese Clothing Appreciation Explanation of traditional Chinese clothing and how it has been incorporated into contemporary designs. Blanc de Chine, Room 201 Pedder Building, 12 Pedder St, Central. Wed, 1430-1530.

Duk Ling Ride One-hour ride on the only authentic Chinese junk boat still sailing in Hong Kong. Recommended, advance reservations strongly advised. Boarding from Kowloon Public Pier, Tsim Sha Tsui (left of Star Ferry) Thu, 1400 and 1600; from Queen's Pier, Central, Thu, 1500 and 1700.

Feng Shui Makes some sense of the 3000 year-old science, invaluable for seeing buildings in a new light. Recommended. Flat C, 14/F Golden Hill Commercial Building, 39-41 Argyle St, Mongkok. Thu, 1030-1130.

Guided Architecture Tour Walk through Central district led by an architect, explaining special characteristics of the old and new buildings. HKTB Visitor Information and Services Centre, G/F The Center, 99 Queen's Rd, Central. Sat, 1000-1300.

Kung Fu Corner Learn the different styles of Kung Fu, with demonstrations, displays and participation. Great for kids. Sculpture Walk, Kowloon Park, Tsim Sha Tsui. Sun, 1430-1630.

Tai Chi Class Learn the practice of the ancient martial art of Tai Chi, alongside other participants and explained by experts. Piazza, Hong Kong Cultural Centre, Tsim Sha Tsui. Mon, Wed, Thu and Fri, 0800-0900.

Other cultural tours

The **Land Between Tour** covers parts of the New Territories including traditional temples, travel to the top of Hong Kong's highest mountain, and a bird sanctuary near the China border. Daily, morning departure, 4½ hours, pick up from Mandarin Oriental Hotel, Central, and Kowloon Hotel, Tsim Sha Tsui. **Heritage Tour** includes Tai Po Market and Man Mo Temple, Tang Chung Ling Ancestral Hall, Lo Wai walled village and Wishing Trees. For tours operated by HKTB, book with them, **T** 2508 1234, or through hotel concierge.

Tourist information

The extremely efficient **Hong Kong Toutist Board**, **T** 2508 1234, www.discoverhongkong.com, *0800-1800 daily*, is a helpful organization, with both good literature and website. There is a huge range of leaflets in English and staff can usually answer even the most obscure questions, help with booking tours, accommodation, shopping and eating, and sell museum passes.

Visitors' centres

NB All offices have the same contact number: **T** 852 2508 1234.
Airport: Buffer Halls and Transfer Area E2. *0700-2300 daily*. Has a

good range of leaflets and brochures but staff are not always present or particularly helpful.

Hong Kong Island: G/F The Center, 99 Queen's Rd, Central. *0800-1800 daily.* Large office and helpful staff, huge amounts of information. Can arrange tours and help with accommodation, and lend out the audio equipment for the Hong Kong Island self-guided walk.

Kowloon: Star Ferry Concourse, Tsim Sha Tsui. *0800-1800 daily.* Very accessible, with the usual range of information. Audio equipment here for the Kowloon self-guided walk.

Information outside Hong Kong
UK: 6 Grafton St, London W1S 4EQ, **T** 020 7533 7100, lonwwo@hktourismboard.com
USA: 115 East 54th Street 2/F, New York, NY 10022 4512, **T** 1212 421 3382, nycwwo@hktourismboard.com
Suite 2050, 10940 Wilshire Boulevard, Los Angeles, CA 90024 3915, **T** 1310 208 4582, laxwwo@hktourismboard.com
130 Montgomery St, San Fransisco, CA 94104, **T** 1415 781 4587, sfowwo@hktourismboard.com
Canada: 3/F 9 Temperance St, Toronto, Ontario M5H 1Y6, **T** 1417 366 2389, yyzwwo@hktourismboard.com
Australia: Level 4 Hong Kong House, 80 Druitt St, Sydney, NSW 2000, **T** 02 9283 3083, sydwwo@hktourismboard.com

Maps
Most major bookshops will sell decent maps, although there are free ones available from the HKTB. The Hong Kong Directory, a detailed street map with index and public transport timetables, is great for a longer stay. Hiking maps are also available, such as the SCMP hiking guide, and there are maps of the islands and New Territories essential for hiking available from the **Government Publications Centre**, G/F 66 Queensway, Admiralty, **T** 2537 1910. *Mon-Fri 0900-1800, Sat 0900-1300.*

Hong Kong Island

Kowloon

Hong Kong Island

Central and Sheung Wan

Flashing neon, rumble of the tram, sunlight on steel. For most people **Central** *represents the essence of Hong Kong; shiny glass and granite* **skyscrapers** *and the best examples of breathtaking* **architecture**, *glamorous* **shopping centres**, *crowded* **street markets**, *the best selection of international cuisine, and the funkiest bars and clubs. Add to this* **Star Ferry**, *the dazzling lights of the* **harbour**, *a couple of parks and museums, relics of graceful colonial days, and of course the human river of office workers and shoppers. Apart from the Macau Ferry Terminal, Sheung Wan Gala point and a couple of new plazas,* **Sheung Wan** *is best known for its wholesale trade in Chinese medicine and culinary specialities like bird's nest and shark's fin.*

▸▸ *See Sleeping p119, Eating and drinking p135, Bar and clubs p157*

 Sights

★ Star Ferry Pier
0630-2330, every 4-10 mins. Lower deck: $1.70, $1.20 children. Upper deck $2.20, $1.30 children. Map 2, D10, p249 See also p27

It's the journey that everyone does in Hong Kong; one of the most famous and shortest ferry journeys in the world, from Kowloon to Hong Kong Island on the Star Ferry that's been shuttling passengers along the eight-minute ride since 1898. Little has changed except for the relocation of the Central pier in 1952 onto reclaimed land. Each 39-ton double-decker ferry, between Wan Chai and Central to Tsim Sha Tsui and Hung Hom, travels 400 times daily taking around 100,000 passengers, a staggering 35 million passengers a year.

● *The area around Star Ferry pier is lively and functional and there's a good bookshop and a bakery.*

City Hall

7 Edinburgh Pl, Central, **T** 2921 2840, www.cityhall.gov.hk URBTIX Box Office, Foyer, **T** 2734 9009. *Box office 1000-2130. Check the press for details of what's on. MTR: Central. Map 2, F11, p249*

This uninspiring concrete building in two blocks, representing some of the worst civic architecture, was the first multi-purpose cultural community centre in Hong Kong. Since its opening in 1962 it has held over 10,000 local and overseas arts groups with equal emphasis on Eastern and Western cultures. Regarded as one of the cradles of Hong Kong's culture and arts, many groups have flourished since first performing here. The vast complex has a 1470-seater concert hall, 463-seater theatre, recital room, an exhibition gallery, library and memorial gardens. Over the years it has hosted milestone events since the early days of the Hong Kong Festival, the first Hong Kong Arts Festival in 1973, Asian Arts Festival in 1976, Film Festival in 1977 and International Arts Carnival in 1982.

● *There's a good dim sum restaurant on the second floor.*

HSBC

1 Queen's Rd Central. *0900-1630 Mon-Fri, 0900-1230 Sat. Banking halls on 1/F and 2/F. MTR: Central. Map 2, G10, p249*

This high-tech icon, designed by Norman Foster in 1985, is one of Hong Kong's most charismatic buildings and is a marriage of two of the strongest elements of the city: a no-holds-barred approach to architecture and testament to the abiding importance of feng shui. The original HSBC was opened in 1864 and even then considered a progressive landmark. When it was rebuilt in 1935, the two bronze lions at the entrance were the only original feature.

!
● The lions guarding the HSBC are called Stephen and Stitt, after the bank's chief managers in Hong Kong and Shanghai during the 1930s.

When it was rebuilt in the 1980s, it was the first building in Hong Kong to have an all-steel skeleton. It was also the most expensive building in the world, based on unit cost.

Its walkway underneath, with two escalators from street level to enter the bank, could be said to be a waste of valuable space. But this is to allow the spiritual dragon from Victoria Peak, the mountain range behind, to run down Old Peak Road, via Government House and finally to the sea. Incongruous though it seems to the outsider, the Chinese believe that it is because of this strategic calculation and positioning that the bank is so successful.

🔵 *On your way in, bring yourself good luck by stroking a lions' paw.*

Fringe Club

2 Lower Albert Rd, Central, **T** 2521 7251, www.hkfringeclub.com
1200-2400 Mon-Thu, 1200-0300 Fri-Sat, closed Sun. MTR: Central.
Map 2, G7, p249

This red-and-white-striped Edwardian-style building is the focal point of the alternative arts scene, hosting a lively collection of gallery space, small theatre, live music venue, bars and restaurants and workshop, as well as being the brains behind the CityFestival.

Recently declared a heritage monument, it was built around 1890, then renovated in 1913 giving a modern edge to the colonial building. Originally the main depot of the Dairy Farm, it churned out dairy products, smoked meats and ice (hence the adjacent Ice House Street), and when operations moved in 1950, there were plans to demolish the building. In 1982 the Foreign Correspondents Club took over the northern section of the building (a members-only club and haunt of journalists, lawyers and egotists), and the Fringe Club took over the south.

Taking its name from the Edinburgh Fringe Festival, the club was established in 1983 initially as a temporary body to organize a new Fringe Festival. Volunteers cleaned the building and built a bar and theatre and the festival (now called the CityFestival and held annully) was such a popular event that the club has continued to thrive, even though still a non-profit-making organization. It is also a popular venue for food and drinks (see pp140 and 158).

Lan Kwai Fong and D'Aguilar Street
Central. *MTR: Central. Map 2, G6, p248*

The small rectangle formed by these two small streets is the nucleus of the hippest and most popular nightlife in Hong Kong. Of course those on the scene will swear that LKF is passé, and that SoHo is *the* place to be, but if you are looking for a condensed area of bars, restaurants, cafés and clubs popular with the young professional, then this is a good area to trawl around. By day it still buzzes, especially with workers on lunch break and with shoppers from the busy Queen's Road. Catch an interesting view of the street from the **Lan Kwai Fong Gallery**, *1/F no 5-6*. Half way up D'Aguilar Street on the right hand side is **Wing Wah Lane** with restaurants, bars and people spilling out onto the grubby courtyard on hot Friday nights.

Bank of China
1 Garden Rd, Central. *0900-1700 Mon-Fri, 0900-1400 Sat. MTR: Central or Admiralty. Tram. Map 2, H11, p249*

Soaring 368 m high and the world's fifth tallest building, the Bank of China is one of the most gracious and elegant of all the towers along Hong Kong's waterfront, and its dynamic geometry is exciting to look at from all angles. Built by American-Chinese architect IM Pei and completed in 1989 around the time of the joint declaration, it was always going to be a prominent landmark designed to represent the aspirations of the Chinese people. The 70-storey tubular structure is built in four triangular glass-and-steel shafts, with an oriental flavour depicting an emerging stalk of bamboo, representing the growth and strength of the bank. Feng shui experts

Law and architectural order

The sharp corners and geometric lines of the Bank of China juxtaposed with the colonial structure of the LEGCO building.

compare it unfavourably with HSBC, reckoning that the lack of open space in front and the Anti Corruption unit on the top floor of the opposite building, spell out relative disaster.

Hong Kong Park and Aviary

19 Cotton Tree Dr, Admiralty. *MTR: Admiralty. Park: 0630-2300. Aviary: 0900-1700. Map 2, H11, p249*

A sensitive piece of landscaping in the midst of Central's traffic and skyscrapers, this well laid-out garden, covering an area of more than 10 hectares of densely wooded land, features the impressive Edward Youde aviary, waterfall, playground, artificial lake and rock garden. Its sheer size is impressive, plus the fact that it succeeds so well as an urban park, providing space and nature to a city living and working in congested conditions. It also houses the registry office, thereby providing the perfect location for scenic wedding photos. The aviary has a wonderful collection of 150 species of Southeast Asian birds and is also a design masterpiece, made from gracefully curved arches of cable and wire mesh.

Flagstaff House Museum of Tea Ware

Hong Kong Park, 10 Cotton Tree Dr, Central, **T** 2869 0690, www.lcsd.gov.hk/hkma *1000-1700, closed Tue. MTR: Admiralty.*
Map 2, H12, p249

Flagstaff House is inside the park, a delightful colonial-style building built in 1844, and once home to the commander-in-chief of the British Forces, Major General George Charles D'Aguilar. An attractive, white, open front with pillars and surrounded by gardens, it is one of the oldest surviving colonial buildings in the territory. It contains the world's largest collection of Chinese porcelain and earthenware tea ware from different periods, donated by Dr K S Lo, and which all looks very much at home in the elegant high-ceilinged interior.

Botanical and Zoological Gardens

Albany Rd, Central. *Map 2, H7, p249*

Near the former British governor's residence, these gardens were the brainchild of a nature-loving governor and completed in 1864. Like most green expanses in the city centre, they are a popular gathering for morning tai chi practitioners. For the later risers, it is also a lovely shady spot with a fountain, well-kept lawns, and an aviary containing myriad birds including bright pink flamingos and ducks. On the other side of Albany Road are the zoological gardens, a less pleasant affair with a few miserable primates in small cages.

Statue Square

Chater Rd, Central. *MTR: Central. Map 2, F10, p249*

The most valuable land in the world, and the most important public space on Hong Kong Island, is looked down upon by the dour statue of Sir Thomas Jackson, once the chief manager of Hongkong Bank. Every Sunday and public holiday the square is filled to the brim with flocks of Filipino domestic workers on their one precious day off, gossiping, eating, singing and doing manicures. HSBC granted crown leases for the land for 999 years, and since 1901 it has been decreed a permanent public space.

Legislative Council (LEGCO)

Chater Rd, Central. *MTR: Central. Map 2, G10, p249*

It is refreshing to see an impressive reminder of colonial times still standing amidst futuristic chrome and glass, and this symbol of British rule is seen as a historical monument (complete with the Royal Arms and Tudor crown which have been allowed to remain). A neo-classical Greek structure with neo-Grecian faces and 15 bays with columns, and the blindfolded statue of Justice, it was previously the Supreme Court and built in the late 19th century. After the new courts were built in Queensway, this became Hong Kong's nearest thing to the Houses of Parliament, the Legislative Council. On the eastern side is Chater Garden, once the location of the Hong Kong Cricket Club, where matches took place on one of the most prominent colonial points in the territory.

Exchange Square

8 Connaught Pl, Central. *MTR: Central. Map 2, D8/9, p249*

The three towers of the pink, Spanish granite and silver reflective glass are a striking sight when emerging from the Star Ferry and walking into Central. The three towers, containing the Hong Kong

Central scene
Busy street stalls contrast sharply with surrounding skyscrapers – a common sight in this part of Hong Kong island.

Stock Exchange, cover an astounding area of 13,400 square metres and have a daytime population of around 16,000 people. The Central Bus Station covers the entire ground floor and the main entrance to the public plaza is dominated by a huge sculpture by Henry Moore. All this is linked by walkway over Connaught Road Central and Des Voeux Road Central to join the mid-levels escalator.

The Lanes and Pottinger Street

Li Yuen St East and West, Pottinger St. *MTR: Central.*
Map 2, E7, p249

These alleyways, running between Des Voeux Road and Queen's Road Central, are a typical example of how much activity can be packed into such a small space. A hive of noise, consumerism, cheap clothes and naff watches lie between dark grubby buildings with dripping air conditioners. But hold on to your hat and plough through the crowds. Everything is here, from knickers the size of small buses to fake Shanghai Tang jackets (at a tenth of the price of the original). Pottinger Street is next to Li Yuen Street West and its steps are lined with booths selling buttons, bows and ribbons.

Stanley Street and Graham Street

Central. *MTR: Central.* *Map 2, F7, p249*

Probably the best area in Hong Kong to buy reliable photographic equipment, Stanley Street runs between D'Aguilar and Graham streets, a narrow road always congested with people and minibuses. Continue from the photographic shops and the atmosphere changes to one of eating, as tables and chairs are arranged haphazardly and cheap, filling Chinese and Vietnamese food is served up to office workers. A left turn at the end brings you to a lively little fruit and vegetable market along Graham Street, where you might catch a butcher stitching up a freshly gutted chicken, or boxes of stripy salted duck eggs amongst the pak choi and potatoes. In the middle is Yung Lee Hong (no 26), a shop with interesting curios towards the back, past the initial junk, like old abacuses and porcelain pieces.

Mid-Levels Escalator and SoHo
Down 0600-1020, up 1020-2400. Map 2, F5, p248

The 800m-long series of covered escalators supposedly eases traffic congestion from the residential area south of Hollywood Road and below the peak, as commuters instead stand on the world's longest covered escalator system and make the journey down to Central. After 1020 the direction changes, and until midnight the escalators travel uphill, giving everyone an easy view into alleyways and shops. It has also led to the development of fashionable new bars, clubs and restaurants, with the emphasis on international cuisine, around Elgin, Staunton, Shelley, Peel, Old Bailey and Cochrane streets. The first five are now known as SoHo (South of Hollywood Road) which has overtaken Lan Kwai Fong in the 'hippest place to hang out' stakes. The entire journey, between Connaught Road and Robinson Road, takes 20 minutes although if you make use of the 29 handy entry and exits points, can take a pleasurable couple of hours.

● *Just off the Mid-levels escalator is a culinary highlight: 32 Lyndhurst Terrace, favourite haunt of former governor Chris Patten. He regularly popped in for his fix of freshly baked egg tarts.*

St John's Cathedral
4-8 Garden Rd, Central. *0700-1800.* Map 2, H10, p249

Tucked away around the back of Queen's Road Central, the cathedral is the oldest surviving western ecclesiastical building in Hong Kong, and thought to be the oldest Anglican church in the Far East. During the Japanese occupation, however, it was used as a social club and suffered severe damage during World War II. Built in 13th-century Gothic style, it was completed in 1849 under

Bishop George Smith. An eastern extension was added in 1873, the foundation stone of which was laid by the Duke of Edinburgh.

Government House

Upper Albert Rd, Central. Enquiries **T** 2530 2003. *Usually closed, save for the occasional concert, although the rhododendron-filled gardens are open for a few days in early spring.* *Map 2, H8, p249*

A Georgian-style mansion with a rather incongruous Japanese turret added on during the Japanese occupation to take the edge off the overwhelming colonial flavour, this was the official residence of all the Hong Kong Governors between 1855 and 1997. Chris Patten was the last governor to reside there as Tung Chee-hwa, the Chief Executive since 1997, prefers to live in his house in Magazine Gap Road (apparently because of bad feng shui). It's strange to think, when taking into account the surrounding towers at close proximity, that this once enjoyed a harbour view.

University Museum and Art Gallery

University of Hong Kong, 94 Bonham Rd, Central, **T** 2241 5500, www.hku.hk/hkumag *0930-1800 Mon-Sat, 1330-1730 Sun. Tea Gallery 1000-1700 Mon-Sat, 1400-1700 Sun, closed on public holidays.* *Map 1, C2, p247*

Next to the University's main entrance, the museum is in the beautiful old Fung Ping Shan Building, donated in 1932 for use as a library and converted into a museum in 1963. Between that and the new wing in the TT Tsui Building, a rather less attractive red-brick tower joined by a bridge, the collection includes over 1000 Chinese antiquities. The bronzes date from the Shang (c. 1550-1030 BC) and Tang (c. 618-906 AD) Dynasties, carvings are in jade, wood and stone, and there are ceramics and Chinese oil paintings. A lovely addition is the Tea Gallery, which promotes the delicacy and culture of Chinese tea. Sit down and sample some best known varieties.

Man Mo Temple

Hollywood Rd. *Map 2, D2, p248*

Man Mo Temple was built in 1847 and like all Man Mo temples
throughout Hong Kong and China, it honours the gods of literature
(Man, dressed in green) and war (Mo, dressed in red), two of the
most worshipped gods in ancient China. The air is usually thick with
the smell and smoke from incense sticks and coils, considered to be
food for the spirits, which is why they are always kept burning.
During the Qing Dynasty (1644-1912), legal disputes were settled
here. There is an ornately carved door at the entrance and three
altars, usually with a slow stream of worshippers praying to the the
gods, burning paper money or incense. The temple's exterior and
colourful carved roof, juxtaposed against grey tower blocks, is one of
those priceless images so representative of Hong Kong life.

★ Cat Street, Hollywood Road and Wyndham Street

Between Central and Sheung Wan. Map 2, D2, p248

Opposite Man Mo temple is Ladder Street, a set of steps which
descend to Upper Lascar Row, commonly known as Cat Street, a
tiny open-air curio market and crammed with a plethora of eclectic
souvenirs and gifts, usually entailing an awful lot of enjoyable
rummaging. The steps leading to Lok Ku Road offer an interesting
mix of second-hand golf clubs, old clocks and the kind of clothes
not seen since the 1950s.

Hollywood Road, built by the British Army in 1844, is the heart of
Hong Kong's antique, curio and handicraft shops, with imports
from China and Southeast Asia (see p189). It's possible to pick up
(not literally) a life-size terracotta warrior, 100-year old temple
carvings, antique beads, Ming furniture and Chinese prints. It's a
relatively quiet street, which is a rare delight in Hong Kong.

Heading southeast, on the right, is the **Central Police Station**,
a huge grey building with imposing Doric-style columns built in

1864 with additions from the early 20th century. Around the corner on Arbuthnot Road is the former **Central Magistracy**, another declared monument, dating back to 1847. Wyndham Street, the continuation of Hollywood Rd, has a few decent carpet shops, with goods imported from India, Iran and China.

Sheung Wan Gala Point
Behind bus terminal, Sheung Wan. *1800-0200 Mon-Fri, 1100-0200 Sat-Sun and public holidays. MTR: Sheung Wan, exit D.*
Map 2, A5, p248

With the refreshingly unsophisticated atmosphere of a funfare without the rides, the Sheung Wan Gala Point is a slightly tacky but fun revival of the *dai tat dei*, the so-called poor man's nightclub of the 1960s and 70s. Then, people gathered by the harbour to browse at the night market, eat cheap food and watch free entertainment. Reopened in late 2002, it has more than 265 stalls selling cheap junk, none of your tourist-friendly souvenirs here – this is for local families buying household goods, toys and cheap

Exchanging views
Post-modern subtlety in Exchange Square. Home of the stock exchange. **49**

jewellery. The highlight is the food area with a row of stalls selling fresh seafood: huge prawns, oysters, squid, mussels, plus the usual pig lung and beef dumplings, all great value. (See p140.) The main stage has free local entertainment several nights a week, with drama, music and comedy (mainly in Chinese).

Western Market
323 Des Voeux Rd Central. *1000-1900. MTR: Sheung Wan.*
Map 2, A/B2, p248

Built in 1906, this four-storey red-brick Edwardian building used to be a wet market (fish, meat, fruit and vegetables) and managed to escape demolition during the development boom when the British Government stepped in to restore it. Its attractive exterior has remained, the building given monument status, and the inside was renovated in 1991 as an arts and crafts market. Although rather sanitized with piped music, faux wood signs and a few twee craft shops, it is a good place to shop for fabrics. Gathered around the first floor are a few Shanghai tailors, previously trading on Wing On Street. The entire top floor houses the time warp that is **Treasure Inn Seafood Restaurant**, with its afternoon tea dances, complete with glitter ball and coloured lights. It's easy to wander across the dance floor without realizing, until a waiter will gently move you on. Decorated in traditional Shanghai style, there are live performances of Chinese Opera, which is extremely rare for Hong Kong.

● *On the ground outside the Connaught Road Central entrance, a plaque marks the site of a time capsule, commemorating the market's renovation in December 1990.*

Man Wa Lane, Wing Lok Street and Ko Shing Street
Sheung Wan. *MTR: Sheung Wan   Map 2, B4, p248*

Man Wa Lane, a small alleyway between Bonham Street and Des Voeux Road Central, is lined with tiny booths making and selling chops, or personalized stamps, hand carved from rubber or soapstone – traditionally the most expensive ones are made from ivory or bone. Many of them have beautiful designs carved onto the handle, and are works of art in themselves. Here you can get your name translated into Chinese, or whatever you request. They can be completed within around half an hour, and cost between $60-$150, depending on the size and quality of the handle, and come with a small printing pad and ink. **Wing Lok** and **Ko Shing Streets** are typical of Sheung Wan – traditional Chinese shophouses and warehouses selling a plethora of ingredients to increase energy, cure fevers or generally improve well-being. The ingredients for these are either derived from plants, like ginseng, or body parts of animals – deer antler and bear penis are two examples – and there are those specializing in bird's nest and shark's fin. Nearly all the streets are piled high with goods, some are more innocuous like dried fungus.

Wan Chai

*In the old days, Wan Chai was dominated by the downright sleazy and although the area has cleaned up its act over the years – this is one of the best areas for entertainment and shopping – it's still more earthy than Central and buzzing day and night. **Lockhart Road**, once the red-light district and legendary from its Suzy Wong days, has bars, clubs and restaurants plus a few hostess clubs and love hotels, while the parallel **Hennessy Road** is a thrift-shopper's heaven with dozens of small shops piled with knock-down designer gear – whose labels may or may not be genuine. The area nearer the **harbour** is home to huge institutions like the Convention and Exhibition Centre and the Academy for Performing Arts, plus one of the tallest and most kitsch skyscrapers in the world, **Central Plaza**.*

▸▸ See Sleeping p119, Eating and drinking p141, Bars and clubs p161

◉ Sights

Central Plaza
18 Harbour Rd, Wan Chai. *MTR: Wan Chai. Map 3, D9, p251*

Hong Kong's skyline contains the tasteful, the tedious and the downright tacky. Central Plaza is undeniably one of the most glitzy and garish buildings – all 78 storeys of it – in the territory. Its golden façade is reflected inside with over ornate decor and a huge, kitsch green marble motif at the entrance lobby, complete with mammoth palm trees. Finished in 1992, the plaza is a convenient walkway between the Convention and Exhibition Centre and Immigration Tower, and has the bonus of a public viewing gallery on the 46th floor.

Old Wan Chai Post Office
221 Queen's Rd East, Wan Chai. *MTR: Wan Chai. Map 3, H8, p251*

This beautiful old post office, in the heart of Wan Chai and all its chaotic little shops, was built in 1913 and is the oldest post office in Hong Kong. It was turned into an Environmental Resource Centre in 1993 and is the first of its kind here, aiming to encourage environmental awareness and ethics, although judging by people's littering of the country parks, they have their work cut out for them.

Hopewell Centre
183 Queen's Rd East, Wan Chai. *Map 3, H7, p251*

While it appears like any other office block (and it is) this one has the advantage of a glass lift which travels on the outside of the building. Even if you decline the opportunity of afternoon tea at the revolving restaurant (see p142) you can enjoy a couple of minutes travelling 40 floors while secretly wishing the lift would break down. ● *Take the regular lift from 3/F and change at 17/F to see the whole of Wan Chai beneath your feet until 57/F.*

Hong Kong Design Centre
28 Kennedy Rd, Wan Chai, **T** 2522 8688, www.hkdesigncentre.org
1000-1900, closed Sun and public holidays. MTR: Wan Chai.
Map 3, H2, p250

In addition to the range of design-related exhibitions since 2001, the Design Centre is an attraction in itself with a colourful history. It was built in 1896, then owned by the Indochine Bank in 1905, and occupied by the Japanese during the Second World War. It was returned to the Hong Kong Government in 1954 and since then has been used as a variety of educational establishments, and then by the Sino-British liaison group prior to the handover in 1997.

Hong Kong Convention and Exhibition Centre
1 Expo Dr, Wan Chai, **T** 2582 888. *MTR: Wan Chai.* *Map 3, C8, p251*

Sitting on the Wan Chai waterfront is one of the world's largest exhibition and convention centres. The stunning building has sweeping sails and huge glass windows, with a 40,000 sq m aluminium roof representing a seabird soaring into flight. It was the site of the 1997 handover, an event commemorated in the adjacent Bauhinia Square. The centre hosts trade shows, concerts and plays in its two convention halls and two theatres. Among the several cafés and restaurants, the Port Café has 270° views.

Golden Bauhinia
Expo Promenade, Wan Chai. *Map 3, A8, p251*

Built to commemorate the handover of power to China, the Golden Bauhinia, the emblem of post-colonial Hong Kong and on all coins and stamps, is a huge statue adjacent to the Convention and

Exhibition Centre. Every morning sees the pomp and ceremony of the flag-raising parade, which takes place at 0750 performed by five officers in police uniform, to the National Anthem. On special days (1st, 11th and 21st of every month) the ceremony is carried out by officers in ceremonial dress, a rifle escort team and the police band.

Causeway Bay, Happy Valley and North Point

East of Wan Chai, Causeway Bay is one of the most concentrated areas of consumerism on the island, as well as the most crowded and polluted. Chic Japanese department stores sell the best imported food and cramped stalls are laden with Hello Kitty watches. **Times Square** *is a neon-flashing shopping centre into which most of Hong Kong descends in the evenings and also a good area to rest weary feet and eat. Happy Valley is dominated by the* **racecourse**, *a highlight of everyone's holiday, especially the sight of the brilliant green track surrounded by dull grey concrete at night. Further east towards North Point it's less prestigious and commercial and more traditional.*

▸▸ *See Sleeping p121, Eating and drinking p143, Bars and clubs p162*

◉ Sights

Happy Valley Racecourse
Happy Valley, **T** 1817, www.happyvalleyracecourse.com *Wed evenings 1930-2230 Dec-Jun. MTR: Causeway Bay, or tram.*
Map 4, H3, p252

The racecourse was built on reclaimed marshland and hosted its first races in 1846, so it's something of a Hong Kong institution. Today the course is one of the most sophisticated in the world with computerized betting and races broadcast on enormous screens.

For many people a night at the races is a highlight and if gambling is not a priority, the roar of the crowds and the thundering of hoofs, are entertainment enough. Otherwise it's a good, cheap night out – providing you don't throw too much money at the Hong Kong Jockey Club, the only legal gambling outlet in the city. Minimum bet is $10, and the small betting cards are tricky for the novice although staff are happy to explain the different combinations (quinella, trifecta etc). It isn't always easy to get the odds at the ground – the complicated screen has confusing lists of numbers – but go armed with the Racing section of the *South China Morning Post* and look like an expert. The biggest races of the year are the **Hong Kong International Races** (December) and the **Queen Elizabeth II Cup** (April).

The public enclosure costs $10, with the option of watching the races at ground level or sitting in the terraces. On production of a passport, foreign tourists may sit in the members' enclosure for $50, closer to the winning post but more restrained and plush. The public enclosure has a few stalls selling chicken's feet, pork chops, hot dogs and noodles, and beer is available from there or from the furtive sellers with large shopping bags. For something more exotic, dine at the trackside Moon Koon Restaurant, or the stable bend terrace with a barbecue buffet, both costing $288 each. Bookings must be for a minimum of four people but two people can book on the day.

Hong Kong Racing Museum

2/F Happy Valley Stand, Happy Valley Racecourse, **T** 2966 8065. *1000-1700 Tue-Sun and some public holidays, 1000-1230 racedays, closed Mon and some public holidays. MTR: Causeway Bay, or tram. Map 4, H2, p252*

Opened in 1996, the museum tells the story of Hong Kong's racing scene, from its early years in the 1840s, through the building of the Sha Tin course and up to the present-day high-tech wonders.

Noon Day Gun and typhoon shelter

Opposite Excelsior Hotel, Causeway Bay typhoon shelter. *Gun fired daily 1200.* Map 4, B5, p252

One of the most charismatic colonial relics, still firing away, is the Noon Day Gun – keeping alive Noel Coward's lines from *Mad Dogs and Englishmen*: "In Hong Kong, They strike a gong, And fire off a noonday gun, To reprimand each inmate, Who's in late." The short ceremony still gathers a small crowd, all guaranteed to cover their ears and giggle as the boom echoes across the water. The typhoon shelter is hardly picturesque, but there are houseboats with washing lines and plant pots, and some more elaborate junk boats and yachts belonging to members of the adjacent Royal Hong Kong Yacht Club. The odd dead fish in the murky water indicates its filth and the summertime stench gives a whole new meaning to the words 'Fragrant Harbour' (translation of Hong Kong).

Take a closer look at life on the water by flagging down a **sampan** (see p28) from the Noon Day Gun steps, pointing your index finger down and making a stirring motion. This will give you a 15-minute trip around the shelter (check the price first, $40-50 for the boat is a reasonable amount, and don't be surprised if you pick up other locals). Watch out for the gin palaces, tour boats, junks and the tiny rowing boats that people actually live on, plus a floating Tin Hau temple – fantastic during the Tin Hau festival, see p181.

Jardine's Crescent

Causeway Bay. *MTR: Causeway Bay.* Map 4, E5/6, p252

This area of Causeway Bay is not for the faint-hearted. It's possibly the most crowded, congested and polluted area of Hong Kong with a high volume of department stores, hotels and markets and it's a natural meeting point for many other parts of the city. Step out into Jardine's Crescent from a sassy department store or the MTR and you are instantly hit with a slow-moving sea of people along the narrow market street. Like the rest of Causeway Bay, the stalls stay open until late evening and, like many other street markets, it mainly sells cheap clothes, Hello Kitty watches, buckets and brooms and plastic jewellery. The dazzling lights of the neon and bright covers contrast with the looming grey buildings.

Victoria Park
Gloucester Rd/Causeway Rd/Victoria Park Rd, Causeway Bay. *MTR: Causeway Bay. Map 4, B6, p253*

One of Hong Kong's largest public parks, in the heart of Causeway Bay, Victoria Park has swimming pools, a football pitch, running tracks and tennis courts. As at most open areas, tai chi practitioners gather every morning and just watching them brings a feeling of calm amidst the chaos. The park's highlight is during Lunar New Year, when a flower show covers a huge area of the park, featuring exotic flowers from here and abroad. The evening before the first day of New Year it's open all night, a seething mass of Hong Kongers buying flowers for their house and the temple. Annually on June 4 a vigil commemorates the events at Tiananmen Square in 1989.

● *Let your weary feet go naked and walk around the oval-shaped foot massage path, covered with specially selected massage stones designed for stimulated circulation, and barefoot walking heaven.*

Chun Yeung Street and Marble Street
North Point, tram or MTR. Map1, C5, p247

Try North Point for a taste of a traditional Chinese street market without the crowds of Mongkok or Wan Chai. Chun Yeung Street, where the tram runs down, has a fish, meat and vegetable market on one side and ultra cheap clothes opposite. At the end, under the flyover, it continues onto Marble Street with some interesting shops like No 10D (selling frogs and snakes, live of course). Further down, incense, candles and tiny wooden statues are for sale.

Sun Beam Cinema

423 King's Rd, North Point, **T** 2856 0161, 2856 0162. *MTR or tram, North Point. Map 1, C5, p247*

For the most authentic Cantonese Opera experience, this cinema has performances most evenings starting at 1930 and lasting up to three hours, with tickets costing between around $100 to $300. Although nothing is in English, it makes for an unusual and enjoyable night out, especially after visiting the Chinese Opera exhibition in the Heritage or History museums. The tiny ground floor stall sells cassettes and posters of popular opera stars.

Shau Kei Wan, Sai Wan Ho and Chai Wan

This area of northeast Hong Kong Island has a couple of interesting museums, including the new Hong Kong Film Archive, although there is little else to keep you here for long. En route to the **Museum of Coastal Defence** *from Shau Kei Wan (either MTR or the last stop on the tram) visit the* **T'ien Hau Temple** *on Shau Kei Wan Main Street East, built in 1873, and the more modern* **Shing Wan Temple** *on Kan Wa Street.*
▸▸ *See Eating and drinking p144*

 Sights

Museum of Coastal Defence

175 Tung Hei Rd, Shau Kei Wan, **T** 2569 1500. *1000-1700. Closed Thu. $10, $5 children. Wed free. Map 1, C7, p247*

Popular with children, this museum was built on the site of the Lei Yue Mun Fort overlooking Shau Kei Wan typhoon shelter and Kowloon. You are greeted with British-made armoured personnel carriers, originally belonging to the Royal Hong Kong regiment. The main building on the 8/F has displays of Hong Kong's maritime history neatly divided into the major periods like Ming, Qing, First Opium War, British Period and Japanese Occupation, each with huge illustrations and life-size models. There is also a small exhibition on the life of Dr Sun Yat Sen (recognized as China's modern founding father and leader of the insurrection against Qing dynasty), an underground battery with the original carved stone floor and the depression range finder where telescopes once stood to see across the bay. A small café has drinks and simple meals and the path back down the hill has been made into a historical trail. ●*Turn down the nearby A Kung Ngam Village Road to the minuscule Yuk Wong Temple, where a small cluster of tin shacks give a great impression of Hong Kong's past, before everyone lived in concrete blocks.*

Hong Kong Film Archive

50 Lei King Rd, Sai Wan Ho, **T** 2739 2139, www.filmarchive.gov.hk *Main exhibition hall: 1000-2000. Box office: 1200-2000. Resource centre: 1000-1900 Mon-Fri, 1000-1700 Sat, 1300-1700 Sun and public holidays, closed Thu. Map 1, C6, p247*

This wonderful centre was opened in January 2001 and is dedicated to preserving Hong Kong's film heritage with an expansive collection of films and artefacts and by holding regular seminars, retrospectives and festivals to promote film. The 3/F Resources Centre houses over 4,300 films, plus thousands of books, magazines and audio-visual material, and four individual viewing booths ($50/day). The ground floor has a large gallery, usually the work of contemporary local artists or photographers, proving that art can be displayed in an innovative and original way.

● *Although hardly noticeable, there is a tiny display next to the information counter selling books of postcards (beautiful collections of images) on Hong Kong Martial Art Movies, The Early Days of Hong Kong Cinema and Film Archive Treasures, costing between $10-20.*

Law Uk Folk Museum

*14 Kut Shing St, Chai Wan, **T** 2896 7006. MTR: Chai Wan. 1000-1300
and 1400-1800 Mon-Wed and Fri-Sat, 1300-1800 Sun and some public
holidays, closed Thu and some public holidays. Map 1, D7, p247*

Within walking distance of the Museum of Coastal Defence, the Folk
Museum was converted from a restored 18th-century Hakka village
house and Law Uk (literally 'Law's House'), is the last of its kind in
Chai Wan. The Law family bought it during the Qing Dynasty, a
typical Hakka house with its back to the mountain and its front
facing the sea, although now, of course, with the widespread
reclamation the area is now landlocked. The interior is based around
a central hall, the bedrooms and loft at the sides and it has all been
furnished with authentic village furniture and farming tools.

The Peak

*Peak Tram, or bus no 15 from Central Bus station, City Hall, Queen's
Rd East. Every 15-20 mins, $9.20. Minibus no 1 from Star Ferry pier,
every few mins, $7.50.*

*The Peak justifies its position as one of Hong Kong's most popular
attractions. The highest point in the territory (552 m) has the best
views of the harbour, and also some of the most valuable property in
the world. In the mid-19th century, the wealthier British arrivals
preferred to build their summer houses in the cool, lofty heights of the
Peak rather than on low-lying swampy marshland. Before the days of
buses and taxis, access was by sedan chair only, and ever since then
the Peak has been the exclusive haunt of the territory's elite. Getting
there now includes a ride on the famous **Peak Tram**, although a more
conventional method is by bus (top deck at the front), which in many
ways is more enjoyable. The meandering route through Wan Chai,
snaking above Happy Valley, past the Khalsa Diwan Sikh temple,*

overlooking the Chinese cemetery, then hugging the hillside along
Stubbs Road offers a longer, more leisurely look at the stunning views,
watching them slowly unfold.

▸▸ *See Eating and drinking p144*

◉ Sights

The Peak Tram
Terminal at Garden Rd, Central. *MTR: Central. Free shuttle bus from*
Star Ferry Pier. $30 return, $20 single. 0700-2400, every 15 mins.
Map 2, H10, p247

The oldest and most dramatic way of ascending the Peak is by a
7-minute journey on the Peak Tram. The cable-hauled funicular
railway has been tugging people on a near-perpendicular angle up
the mountainside since 1888 before the roads were ever built, and
transports around 9,000 passengers a day. It is possible to board
and leave the tram from any one of its other four terminals
(Kennedy Road, MacDonnell Road, May Road and Barker Road).

The Peak Tower and Peak Galleria
Map 1, D2, p247

Once at the bus or tram terminal, there are various things you can
do: walk to the very top of the Peak, shop, eat, or just gaze at the
harbour from the viewing platform. The Peak Tower, which looks like
an orange segment from the side, is the tram terminal and also a

! In 2003 Madame Tussaud's at the Peak Tower launched a
• $600 "Star Studded Love Package" for Valentine's Day, which
gave locals the chance to propose in front of their favourite
celebs. The deal included a long-stemmed rose, champagne,
chocolate and a wax cast of the lovers' entwined hands.

multi-purpose viewing, dining and entertainment centre, designed by British architect Terry Farrell. While it seems pointless to have a viewing platform when a short walk around the peak reveals it all, it has the advantage of high-powered binoculars. The tower includes the Peak Explorer, Madame Tussaud's and Ripley's Believe It Or Not Odditorium (see Kids, p220).

Opposite the coloured fountain (lit up at night), above the bus terminal, the **Peak Galleria** is another assortment of shops and restaurants, including Peak Concepts (next to Café Deco), The Hard Rock Café Shop and Wai Tat Industries (32-37 level 1) with an excellent collection of souvenirs and handicrafts at reasonable prices.

Police Museum

27 Coombe Rd, The Peak, **T** 2849 7019. *0900-1700 Wed-Sun, 1400-1700 Tue, closed Mon and public holidays.* Map 1, D3, p247

Housed in the old Wan Chai Gap Police Station, this charts the story of one of the oldest police forces in the world. The Royal Hong Kong Police Force was officially formed in 1841. The exhibits include old photographs, uniforms and guns, plus a display on the Triad criminal gangs, and the intriguing ways in which drugs are smuggled.

Walks around the Peak

Map 1, D2, p247

The most popular and easiest walk is from the Upper Peak Tram station, along Lugard Road and Harlech Road, a footpath around the **circumference of the Peak**. The two-mile walk takes under an hour, although the viewing platforms along the way are tempting for a long, lingering look. Choose a clear day and the views are unforgettable: gleaming skyscrapers and one of the busiest harbours in the world; and the Outlying Islands from around the other side. It also allows a peek into how the other half live and some of the most expensive housing (although most of it

▶ Genesis

While gawping at the houses and calculating how many years it would take to save up for a deposit, look out for the (once) world's most expensive house. **Genesis**, the white house at 23 Severn Road was bought in December 2001 by a mainland Chinese tycoon for $230m – less than half its original purchase price. Four years earlier it set the record value for a single house (since surpassed) when it was sold for $540m, a fair whack even for a 28,000- square-foot mansion complete with indoor pool, ornate Italian trimmings and Greek statues. Its original owner sold it to a holdings company at the height of the property boom, which then turned offers down even higher than the purchase price, hoping to sell to the new chief executive after the handover in 1997. But Tung Chee-hwa chose to stay in his relatively modest abode and the government chose not to buy it, a decision unfortunately coinciding with a collapse in the Asian property market. Desperate times lead to desperate measures and after the bank seized the property, the des res was eventually sold "for investment purposes".

surprisingly unattractive) in the world. Most of the walk is pleasantly tree-shaded, even though much of the area was deforested in the mid-19th century when the Brits arrived.

There are a couple of routes to the top of the Peak and **Victoria Peak Garden** by walking along Harlech Road then turning right onto the path at its junction with Lugard Road. It then makes a small loop known as Governor's Walk, ascending to the pleasant gardens.

There are also well-signposted walks to Pokfulam or Aberdeen on the west coast. It's around one hour along a gentle 3-mile walk to the **Pokfulam Reservoir** (stock up for a picnic at Park 'n' Shop in Peak Galleria), then choose between the stiff walk back or a return journey by bus.

South Hong Kong Island

*The villages scattered around the south of the island are most popular because of their waterfront location, ranging from the traditional fishing village of **Aberdeen** with its junks bobbing around the harbour, to the holiday-friendly **Stanley**, famous for its market. An easy journey from Aberdeen is **Ocean Park**, one of the largest oceanariums in Asia, and with plenty to occupy a full day. **Shek O** is a wealthy expat enclave with a dramatic setting via a breathtaking bus ride and **Repulse Bay** is one of the best beaches in Hong Kong, packed at weekends. All are accessible by bus.*

▶▶ *Eating and drinking p145*

Sights

Aberdeen

*Bus nos 70 or 75 from Central or Admiralty. Ferry (**T** 2815 6063) from here to Yung Shue Wan, via Pak Kok Tsuen, 0600-2100, every couple of hours.   Map 1, E3, p247*

This floating village of junks and fishing boats bobbing in the typhoon shelter is worth a detour if en route to Ocean Park, the Peak or Lamma. Out of the ferry pier and on the left is the **Aberdeen Sampan Company**, which offers sampan tours of the harbour for around $50 per person, for a half-hour cruise. You may well be approached by the assertive old ladies who operate the sampans, so settle a price before departing. The road along the waterfront is hardly an attractive one; past the concrete monstrosity on the right, but then there are the free boats to the **floating restaurants**, which is what drew tourists here in the first place.

   The most famous is Jumbo Floating restaurant, a favourite with tour groups since 1976, with rather over-the-top imperial palace decor. With a capacity of 2,300 and said to be the world's largest floating restaurant, don't expect personal service or an intimate atmosphere and even the food would not be worth going for if it wasn't for the novelty of the garish interior. For a free look at its ornate gold furnishings and the 60 breeds of fish and marine life in the pool (there to be eaten), make use of the free shuttle boat taking people from the waterfront. If you eat there, and are prepared to pay over the odds, take heart that your fellow diners included Queen Elizabeth II and John Wayne. Slightly less ornate is the Tai Pak restaurant, also with a free shuttle boat. Further along the pier is a row of boats selling seafood from piles of crates.

Ocean Park

Aberdeen, **T** 2552 0291, www.oceanpark.com.hk *1000-1800. $180, $90 children. Map 1, F4, p247 See also Kids, p219*

A huge oceanarium and theme park with dolphins, pandas, sharks and rides. Good for kids of all ages and equal amounts of education and pure entertainment.

Stanley

Buses nos 6, 6A, 6X or 260 from Exchange Square in Central, or MTR to Chai Wan and green minibus No 16M. Map 1, G6, p247

This small, seaside village on the south of Hong Kong Island makes for a day trip high on easy-going shopping and eating with a little culture and sightseeing thrown in. Once the favourite spot for the first colonial settlers, it is best known for its daily market, with a fort, cemetery and prison slightly further out, and an air of faded grandeur rather like an English seaside resort.

The **open market** stretches between Stanley New Street and Stanley Market Road, *1000-1900 daily*, with a wide collection of good value silk ties, handbags, shoes, Chinese handicrafts and cheap brand-name clothes (some genuine), usually at fixed prices. Rooting around can unearth some decent bargains and it is a good place to stock up on presents. Weekends are the busiest days, but the crowd is pretty good natured. Along the waterfront and inside the market is a huge selection of places to eat, from noodle bars to refined European cuisine, plus several English-style pubs.

Around the bay and on the right-hand-side of Stanley Main Road is one of the oldest colonial buildings in Hong Kong: the **old police station** was built in 1859 and is now a restaurant. A posting to Stanley was hardly ideal considering the high level of danger from piracy as well as isolation and poor health, but the village became a more desirable seaside resort in the early 20th century.

The elegantly built **Murray House**, near the promenade by Stanley Plaza, was originally built in 1844 for the British Army and situated in Central. It was dismantled in 1982 to make way for the Bank of China tower and, all but forgotten, the pieces lay in storage for many years. They were painstakingly rebuilt brick by brick in its current location in 1998 with a few added modern-day gizmos.

Repulse Bay

Bus nos 6, 6A, 6X, 260 from Exchange Square in Central, and alight at Repulse Bay. Map 1, F5, p247

Hong Kong Island's most popular beach can get ludicrously packed at weekends and has recently been extended. The most prominent sight on the approach by bus is the lurid, pastel-coloured **Repulse Bay Apartments**, its undulating surface reflecting the shape of the surrounding hills and a large, square hole eight storeys high punctured through its middle. This replaced the Repulse Bay Hotel (the only remainder of which is The Verandah, see p145), built in the 1920s and one of the area's most prominent landmarks, venue of choice for celebrity cocktail parties and tea dances and the last stronghold against the Japanese invasion during World War II. It was also later used as a hospital and recuperation centre.

Considering that the apartments have some of the highest rents in Hong Kong, the beach is refreshingly kitsch. The lifeguard's terraces (lifeguard between March and November) have a pair of large statues of two goddesses, Kwun Yum and Tin Hau, adjacent to the changing rooms and showers. Space BBQ Restaurant has a large waterfront terrace, complete with a Wurlitzer CD jukebox with all the best Cantopop tunes. A little further down is Tai Fat Hau with traditional Cantonese dishes like hot and spicy duck's tongue and steamed eel in sweet sauce. During the summer, **wakeboarding** operates from Xtreme Wake Boarding (see Sports, p208).

Shek O

Bus no 9 from Shau Kei Wan MTR (Exit A3) and bus no 309 from Exchange Square (Central), Sun only. Map 1, F7, p247

The bus ride alone is worth the trip; a hair-raising route winding through the hills (top deck front seat essential), past Tai Tam reservoir and great views over to Stanley, usually at breakneck speed. Seen from above, it is picturesque and reminiscent of a traditional Chinese community, contrasting starkly to the millionaires' mansions surrounding the village. Shek O is a favourite for wealthy expats, many of whom will be swinging their golf clubs at the nearby exclusive Golf and Country Club. The village itself has a dramatic setting and the beach is pretty big and clean with powdery white sand, toilets, changing facilities, concrete barbecue pits, benches and a playground. Should you have forgotten your bucket and spade, there are shops around the edge of the car park selling beach accessories, charcoal and forks for barbecues, snacks and drinks. No 87 Shek O Village (in the car park) hires bikes for around $50/day, and is open till late in the summer. If the golf club won't let you in, the next best thing is the obstacle golf course on the beach (see Sports, p205). A couple of miles away is **Big Wave Bay**, a much better beach and very popular with surfers (equipment for hire), and also some Bronze Age rock carvings. Although there are very infrequent buses between Shek O village and the bay, it takes around half an hour to walk.

Kowloon

Tsim Sha Tsui

You need a strong stamina to conquer TST on foot, mainly because of the overwhelming mass of people and shops. Most of the cheapest hotels are around here, including **Chungking Mansions**, *contrasting sharply with the luxury of the* **Peninsula Hotel**. *There is a cluster of excellent museums around the waterfront, the* **History Museum** *being the highlight. Some of the most intense shopping, especially for electrical goods, can be done along the* **Golden Mile**, *the southern end of Nathan Road, although this has been marred by the noisy roadworks which will create havoc for pedestrians until 2005.* **Kowloon Park** *offers some welcome space and the walkway in front of the* **Cultural Centre** *is the best place to get a view of the dazzling beauty of the Hong Kong lights, as well as being a venue for free tai chi lessons. The excellent visitors' centre, one of two in the city, is adjacent to* **Star Ferry pier**.

▸▸ *See Sleeping p68, Eating and drinking p146, Bars and clubs p163*

 ## Sights

Star Ferry Pier
Map 5, L2, p255   See also p37

One of the most famous boat rides in the world – just an 8-minute cruise – leaves from the pier on the southern tip of Kowloon with regular sailings to Central and Wan Chai. This particular pier was built in 1957, five years after the Hong Kong side was finished, although the Star Ferry was initiated in 1842 to provide a crossing for the godown (warehouse) workers who didn't have their own transport. The godowns were demolished in 1904, and after the pier was ruined by typhoon, a new one was built in 1910 and incorporated into the Kowloon-Canton Railway terminus. When the current pier was built in 1957, the KCR moved to Hung Hom, and the clock tower (opened in 1921) is the only remainder of this old terminal.

Next to the pier is Ocean Terminal, a four-storey building conceived in 1962 and the first air-conditioned shopping mall in the city. It was the start of the lucrative Wharf property empire which brought Hong Kong into the modern age.

The Peninsula Hotel
Salisbury Rd. *MTR: Tsim Sha Tsui. Map 5, K4, p255 See also page 146*

Worth a visit even if its prices are out of reach – afternoon tea in the lobby or cocktails in Felix are good options – the Peninsula was completed in 1927 and was the first luxury accommodation in Kowloon. It was initially temporary headquarters for British troops, operated as a hotel a year later and quickly became the focus of the Hong Kong social scene. In 1941 it was the setting for the surrender of the city to the commander of the Japanese army, then the headquarters of the Japanese Governor until 1945. It reopened for business a year later and has since been redeveloped, its most prominent addition being the 30-storey tower in 1994.

Star quality
An eight-minute ferry journey, costing $2, with a million dollar view

Hong Kong Cultural Centre

10 Salisbury Rd, enquiries **T** 2734 2848; box office **T** 2734 2009; reservations **T** 2734 9011; www.hkculturalcentre.gov.hk Tai Chi classes (**T** 2508 1234) in the Cultural Centre piazza. *0800-0900 Mon, Wed, Thu and Fri. Free. MTR: Tsim Sha Tsui.* *Map 5, K3, p255*

One of the largest venues for concerts and theatre, the centre was built on the land formerly occupied by the Kowloon-Canton Railway and hardly had the most auspicious start when described as looking like a huge toilet. The design might still be criticized but its function as home to the Hong Kong Philharmonic Orchestra and Chinese Orchestra is not faulted. Free events are held most Thursdays, *Happy Hour, 1800-1900* and Saturdays, *Family Delights, 1430-1630*, in the main foyer, plus temporary exhibitions in the foyer.

The two-tiered waterfront promenade is equally popular, especially for anyone strolling along at night, for one of the greatest views in the world – Hong Kong Island in all its illuminated glory.

The piazza allows an opportunity, at last, to unravel the mysteries surrounding the ancient art of tai chi, dating back to around the 12th century. Free tai chi classes are conducted by Ms Pandora Wu, one of Hong Kong's best-known practitioners who even performed for Tony Blair on his recent visit.

Hong Kong Space Museum

10 Salisbury Rd, **T** 2721 0226. *1300-2100 Mon and Wed-Fri; 1000-2100 Sat-Sun and public holidays; closed Tue. $10, $5 children. Wed free. Space Theatre $24/32, $12/16 children.* *Map 5, K4, p255*

A hands-on display of space and astronomy with telescopes, videos and exhibits held in the Hall of Space Science and Hall of Astronomy. The Space Theatre has several films daily on the giant Omnimax screen, and children will love this journey to the final frontier.

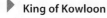

▶ King of Kowloon

Rather than an adolescent lad wearing big trainers and carrying a couple of cans of spray paint, Hong Kong's best-known graffiti artist is a 79-year old man who uses a Chinese calligraphy brush. Not even a crippling accident prevented Tseng Tso-choi from writing his name, plus that of his ancestors, famous historical Chinese and British figures and some not too flattering comments about the Queen, on walls and lamp-posts around town. He has been the subject of documentaries and magazine features and local opinion varies widely as to whether he is working-class hero, eccentric or public nuisance. His own family disowned him, considering him to be mad, but his scribbling has inspired fashion designers, interior decorators and CD cover artists.

Hong Kong Museum of Art
10 Salisbury Rd, **T** 2721 0116, www.lcsd.gov.hk/hkma *1000-1800, closed Thu. $10, children $5, Wed free. Guided tours 1100 and 1600; Sat 1500, 1600 and 1700. MTR: Tsim Sha Tsui, exit E. Map 5, L4, p255*

The Museum of Art's seven exhibition galleries, spread over six floors, contain over 12,000 pieces of art with Hong Kong and Chinese art at its core, divided into five categories of permanent collections including Chinese Painting and Calligraphy and Contemporary Hong Kong art. One of the most popular floors is the Xubaizhai Collection of Chinese Painting and Calligraphy, for which the gallery had to be specially designed and includes works from the Ming and Qing dynasties. The museum also has a Resource Centre, Lecture Hall, studios for ceramics and print-making, a café, *1000-2100*, and bookshop, *1000-1830*.

Nathan Road
Map 5, A-L4, pp254-255

Named after the British Governor who designed it, Nathan Road runs from the southern tip of Tsim Sha Tsui up to Mongkok several miles north. The area dubbed the **Golden Mile** is the most famous, a shopping nucleus, plus cheap hotels and originally scorned as a white elephant, but transformed over the last few decades. The crowds and chaos have been further intensified because of noisy and inconvenient roadworks, due for completion in 2005, restricting pedestrian access and providing an orchestra of pile-drivers and drills. It's also densely populated with touts, eager to sell you a copy watch, the services of a tailor, or a room in a hostel. The streets running off Nathan are a little easier to manage: Mody, Cameron, Granville and Kimberly Roads are some of the best for cheap clothes. Towards Kowloon Park, on the left, is the Parklane Boulevard which has been craftily designed with 370 m of shopfronts, set back from the main road, the sole purpose of which is to slow people down, giving them more time to shop. The street is lined with sturdy banyan trees, best appreciated from the top deck of a bus.

Kowloon Park
22 Austin Rd, Kung Fu Corner **T** 2724 3344. *1430-1630 Sun. MTR: Tsim Sha Tsui. Map 5, G3-4, p255*

With an estimated 60,000 visitors every Sunday, the park is one of Hong Kong's most popular places and its 13.6 hectares a much-needed 'green lung' to compensate for the traffic and activity of Nathan Road. Despite the fact that there is always the sight of a tower block and noise of traffic, at least birds and trees are more prevalent. Previously a military encampment, it was turned into a park after the Second World War and an injection of $300m in 1988 made it one of the most advanced urban parks in the world. With a blissful feeling of space and peace, highlights include a Tai Chi garden, Chinese pavilions, open-air sculpture court, bird lake with swans and teals, adventure playground and an aviary. The **Kung Fu corner** is a big hit with kids (see p218). The outdoor **swimming pools**, *Apr-Oct*, plus indoor Olympic-sized pool and sports centre are also popular (see p207.) In the southeastern corner facing Nathan Road is the serene **Kowloon Mosque and Islamic Centre**, built in the mid-1980s, with marble dome and minarets.

Chungking Mansions
36-44 Nathan Rd. *MTR: Tsim Sha Tsui.* *Map 5, I/J5, p255*

Alongside the relative luxury of the Golden Mile Holiday Inn and the Hyatt, the run down 17-storeys of Chunking Mansions is reminiscent of the shabby chaos of India or Pakistan, but is nonetheless a highly entertaining institution where many of Hong Kong's expatriate workers started out living. Its lower floors are filled with cheap stalls mainly selling Hindi videos, clothes, a few souvenirs, saris and snacks, and the higher floors have some of the cheapest rooms and tastiest Indian food in Hong Kong. There is a 24-hour presence of touts around the ground floor lifts, enticing you to their friend's restaurant or hotel. It can be inconvenient and irritating if you have a venue in mind and need to ask for directions around the confusing blocks – don't be persuaded to make a detour.

Antiquities and Monuments Office
136 Nathan Rd, **T** 2721 2326. *MTR: Tsim Sha Tsui.* *Map 5, E5, p254*

This early-20th-century Victorian Gothic building is a popular backdrop for models, forming a colourful contrast to the neon and urban mediocrity, and a good example of traditional architecture adapted for the local climate. Built in 1902, it was formerly the Kowloon British School, declared a historic monument in 1991 and is now used as an information centre for antiques and monuments. Although little is open to the public, there is a wonderful selection of leaflets specializing in heritage and historical places of interest, especially in the New Territories.

Hong Kong Museum of History

100 Chatham Rd South, Tsim Sha Tsui, **T** 2724 9042. *1000-1800 Mon and Wed-Sat; 1000-1900 Sun and public holidays; closed Tue. $10, $5 children. Free on Wed. Guided tours in English 1030-1430 Sat, Sun and public holidays.* Map 5, E8, p254

One of the finest museums in the city, the Hong Kong Story is the huge, permanent exhibition progressing through local history from 400 million years ago until present day. If time or tolerance is limited, bypass the first section on prehistoric evolution, fossils and archaeologists and head for the sections on fishing villages, clan festivals, a Chinese Opera stage complete with costumes, dragon dances, Japanese occupation and post-97 handover. The most interesting collections are those celebrating popular culture, especially films, TV, Cantopop and the cheap goods produced during the 1960s and 70s. An entertaining and educational experience and wonderful for children. Highly recommended.

Hong Kong Science Museum

2 Science Museum Rd, Tsim Sha Tsui E, **T** 2732 3232. *1300-2100 Mon-Fri; 1000-2100 Sat, Sun and public holidays; closed Thu. $25, $12.50 children. Free Wed.*

This child-friendly collection has three floors of colourful educational hands-on exhibits, illustrating the workings of electricity, robotics, the human body and vehicle technology. There are a few live demonstrations, including a computer theatre demonstrating computerized music. The second floor is devoted to energy and the environment, demonstrating green architecture and recycling and the children's zone with educational toys, is designed for even younger kids with space to run around and a 'space age' café.

Jordan, Yau Ma Tei and Mongkok

The area between Jordan and Yau Ma Tei MTR stations has a series of parallel streets revealing Chinese culture in all its glory and laden with street markets: **Reclamation Street** *sells its produce (snakes, frogs, chickens) live,* **Shanghai** *and* **Saigon Streets** *have shops reflecting traditional ways of life like mahjong parlours, pawnshops, shrines and incense and* **Temple Street** *is famous for its night market. Around the junction of Kansu and Battery streets is the* **Jade Market***, where hawkers sell various shades and qualities of jade. Mongkok has the unenviable record of being one of the world's most densely populated urban areas and the best way to absorb its atmosphere is simply to walk the streets, especially around* **Ladies***,* **Goldfish** *and* **Flower Markets***. Rather than trawling down Nathan Road, which can get rather trying, take the parallel Sai Yeung Choi Street South. Although hardly glamorous or relaxing, Mongkok oozes with life and character, and hotels here are much cheaper than in Tsim Sha Tsui.*

▸▸ *See Sleeping p124 and Eating and drinking p148*

◉ Sights

★ Temple Street Market

Temple St, between Jordan and Yau Ma Tei. *MTR: Jordan 1600-2200. Map 5, A3, p254*

A lot of action in a surprisingly small space, the night market of Temple Street is worth experiencing not just because of the cheap clothes, souvenirs, Chinese clothes and CDs, but for the fringe events to the main attractions. The action gets going in the afternoon but the atmosphere buzzes in the late evening, and given the density of crowds it can take a long time to shuffle between the stalls. Shops also line the street so look out along the pavement for anything you might have missed.

About half way down on the corner with Pak Hoi Street is the **Temple Street Food Store**, a lively food court with a cluster of restaurants on the street and, under cover, serving up Chinese and seafood dishes, a couple of which have English menus. The best ones include Wing Fat Seafood Restaurant and Tak Kee Seafood Restaurant, and Tong Tai Restaurant is on the corner with Ning Po Street. For the more adventurous, 230-236 Temple Street specializes in snake soup, with a sign declaring "good to health during cold weather and alleviates rheumatism. MSG free". The bright, busy café is open till 0200, and for those who weren't sure about the physical construction of a snake, it has a skeleton, complete with ribs, on display on the table. A quieter place to try is at 164 Shanghai Street, where braised snake soup costs $25.

Just to prove that there is a life away from shopping and eating, Temple Street also introduces you to amateur **Cantonese Opera**, or musical recitals on traditional instruments, performed most nights between 2000-2200 along the darkened alley south of the temple. Stop by and listen, and although the elderly musicians may not win awards for talent, it is undoubtedly a more authentic way of experiencing the music than in an auditorium. It is free to listen, but there is a charge of around $10 to take a photograph.

On the market street and around the northern end of Temple Street, indulge in another tradition: having your fortune read. This can be done by palm (around $150), face ($100) or the marginally less scientific method of tiny bird ($30), which hops out of the cage and picks an envelope containing a fable that is then interpreted. Pak Hoi and Kansu Streets is an area selling mainly Nepalese goodies.

Yuen Po Street Bird Garden and Flower Market
Yuen Po St and Flower Market St. *MTR: Mongkok.*

Tiny singing birds are a big favourite with Chinese people who see them as lucky, and it is not unusual to see men taking their caged bird for walks in the park. The garden is a new, purpose-built venue for the gentle trade of buying and selling birds, (previously on Hong Kok Street), decorated in traditional style with courtyards and moon gates. Tiny, chirruping budgies and raucous, squawking parrots, plus all the trimmings like ornate cages, porcelain water dishes, live insects (for food) and decorations are all for sale; birds sell from around $100. Towards the park entrance is a semi-covered area with around 70 stalls with more selection.

● *Around the corner to the garden's entrance is Flower Market Street, devoted to wholesale and retail flower shops, and at its best just before Chinese New Year when most of Hong Kong descends to buy up armfuls of blooms.*

A bird in the hand
Taking the bird for a day out in Mongkok Bird garden and sizing up the competition.

Ladies Market and Goldfish Market

Tung Choi St, Mongkok. *MTR: Mongkok.*

The busy street market has piles of clothes and household goods (although not only for ladies), and the produce, while hardly stylish, is certainly cheap. At the southern end of Tung Choi Street, south of Prince Edward Road West, and the area around Bute Street is the Goldfish Market. Like birds, fish are also a desirable addition to any home, and there are colourful fish of all shapes, sizes and breeds swimming around in tanks and plastic buckets, even tiny crabs in plastic bags, making them look like a prize in a fairground. And to help make the fish feel at home, there is also intricate underwater furniture and fluorescent plastic fish for sale in shops such as Success Aquarium, Chun Hing Carp Specialists and Fortune Fish Co.

Wong Tai Sin, Diamond Hill and Kowloon Tong

Although this area of Kowloon is not of general interest and few would choose to stay here, it does have a couple of places of religious value that are close enough to be visited in a half-day. **Wong Tai Sin Temple** *is one of the most important in Hong Kong, and if you're lucky to catch it during a festival, you will witness thousands of devotees praying to the god of Tin Hau and fervently shaking their fortune sticks.* **Chi Lin Nunnery**, *in Diamond Hill a couple of stations away, is a refreshingly peaceful place with a vegetarian restaurant that's open on Sundays. And, just to get back to basic culture, Kowloon Tong has one of the best shopping centres in the territory,* **Festival Walk** *being a large mall with a great selection of mid-range stores, an icerink, cinemas and restaurants, and nothing like the crowds of Causeway Bay or Wan Chai.*

▶▶ *See Eating and drinking p148*

Wong Tai Sin Temple
Worshippers queue up to offer prayers during Chinese New Year.

Unlucky sticks

While many people get their fortune sticks read at the temple and listen to good, bad or indifferent interpretations, it's not so good if your reading becomes a public event. The Secretary of Home Affairs, Patrick Ho, did the annual ritual to see what the year would bring at a Sha Tin Temple for Lunar New Year 2003, when he prayed for prosperity for Hong Kong in the Year of the Goat. His stick was number 83, which signifies woes, turbulence and a difficult time ahead, not what people wanted to hear with high unemployment and poor economy. Needless to say, Mr Ho's reading was splashed all over the newspapers.

 Sights

★ Wong Tai Sin Temple

Wong Tai Sin Rd, adjoining Upper Wong Tai Sin Estate, **T** 2327 8141. *0700-1730. MTR: Wong Tai Sin, exit B2.*

Even if you are not a temple fan, this really is the one to visit, simply to watch the crowds of devotees, especially during Lunar New Year and Wong Tai Sin's birthday. On these days, thousands will come to make offerings, light incense and walk clockwise around the courtyard, shake their fortune sticks and burn paper money. Founded on the lower slopes of the Kowloon Hills over half a century ago, the temple was named after a shepherd boy who gained immortality through his good deeds and mystical healing powers. Buddhism, Taoism and Confucianism are all practised here.

It is a crowded, colourful spectacle, the most popular in Hong Kong, and famed for its soothsayers – all 160 of them – who sit in little numbered booths in the building adjacent to the temple. Several of them speak English (indicated on the board on the right-hand side of the entrance). Each one will have their fixed rates: around $30 for fortune sticks, $300 for palm reading and $500 for palm and face.

Fortune sticks probably originated from a Taoist practice. Each pot has sticks numbered 1 to 100, each number having a corresponding piece of paper on which is written a historical incident or legend, linked to a philosophical idea. The worshipper shakes the pot hard, whilst thinking deeply of their question, until one stick falls out. The relevant piece of paper is then taken to the soothsayer to be interpreted.

Chi Lin Nunnery

Chi Lin Dr, (northern end), **T** 2354 1604. *0900-1530, closed Wed. Lotus garden: 0630-1900. MTR: Diamond Hill.*

Surprisingly few people make it out to Diamond Hill – a simple and graceful wooden nunnery, that has undergone a multi-million dollar renovation using traditional architecture. It is also the largest building in the world to be constructed using no nails – only wooden dowelling and brackets were used. The 323,000 square foot complex features Tang Dynasty-style architecture dating back to AD 618-907, and is set around a peaceful courtyard with lotus-covered pools. The attractive gardens are open to the public even when the nunnery is closed.

There are four halls of Celestial Kings, with statues of Bhaisajya guru (the Medicine Master), the Goddess of Mercy, the Patriarch Hall with tablets of ancient Buddhist sages, and the Main Hall containing a statue of Sakyamuni Buddha, the founder of Buddhism in India 2500 years ago.

Signs to the exit bring you to the dining hall, a lovely way to end the visit if the timing is right, *Sunday 1100-1600*, with a decent self-service vegetarian restaurant, including hot lunch boxes, run by a bunch of friendly women who could teach the staff at Po Lin Monastery a thing or two about service.

Kowloon Walled City Park

Tung Tsing Rd, Kowloon City, **T** 2716 9962 /2762 2084. *0630-2330. Bus no 1 from Star Ferry Pier, Tsim Sha Tsui, or minibus no 39M from Lok Fu MTR.*

The park is the original site of a walled fort, a rectangular garrison built for a senior Mandarin officer after Hong Kong Island was ceded to the British in 1841. It was used to police the Chinese side of the harbour. When the British took the New Territories in 1898, they forced the Chinese to abandon the fort and, after a legal confusion in which it remained empty, squatters moved in. It gradually evolved into a village behind protective walls with cramped, dirty living conditions but a brisk trade and lack of colonial interference. Flattened by the Japanese during the Second World War, when the walls were torn down, it began a new life with the arrival of hundreds of thousands of Chinese refugees. It was then a no-go area, even for police, rife with crime, drugs and Triads flourishing in its dark alleyways. Chinese and British authorities were forced to clean it up, re-house its 30,000 residents, and eventually the Walled City was torn down by 1992. It has since been transformed into a landscaped park with pavilions, fountains and Garden of Chinese Zodiac, with historical remains including a Qing Dynasty alms house and original stone plaques from the Old South Gate.

Museums and galleries

- **Art Museum**, The Chinese University of Hong Kong, Sha Tin, T 2609 7416. *1000-1645 Mon-Sat, 1230-1730 Sun. Closed public holidays.* In conjunction with the University's Fine Art's Department, its collection of valuable art and archaeological exhibits from China help promote Chinese culture.
- **Flagstaff House Museum of Tea Ware** One of Hong Kong's oldest colonial buildings, p42.
- **Fringe Club** Three small areas of gallery space in the foyer, the bar and the first-floor restaurant, predominantly for local artists and photographers, p39.
- **Hong Kong Arts Centre** Showcase for contemporary arts, with work by major international artists, p174.
- **Hong Kong Design Centre** Beautiful old colonial mansion containing contemporary design-related exhibits, p53.
- **Hong Kong Film Archive** Dedicated to preserving Hong Kong's film heritage, p59.
- **Hong Kong Heritage Museum** Depicting the culture and heritage of the territory using life-size models and interactive displays, p89.
- **Hong Kong Museum of Art** Seven galleries with over 12,600 pieces of art, specialising in Chinese painting and calligraphy, and contemporary Hong Kong art, p71.
- **Hong Kong Museum of History** From prehistoric fossils, life-size models of old fishing boats and dragon dances to the fascinating popular culture from the 1960s, p74.
- **Hong Kong Museum of Medical Sciences** 2 Caine Lane, Mid-Levels. T 2549 5123. Charting the history of Western and Chinese medicine.
- **Hong Kong Racing Museum** Showing past runners and riders, and the story of one of the world's richest racing industries, adjacent to the course, p55.

Museums and galleries

- **Hong Kong Railway Museum** A heritage site with old railway carriages, tracks and engines to explore, p92.
- **Hong Kong Science Museum** Three floors of interactive educational exhibits, very child friendly, p74.
- **Hong Kong Space Museum** Suitable for any wannabe astronauts, the giant Omnimax screen is a highlight, p70.
- **Hong Kong Visual Arts Centre**, Hong Kong Park, 7A Kennedy Rd, Central, **T** 2521 3008. *1000-2100, closed Tue and some public holidays.* Supporting local art, and converted from the former Victoria Barracks. It provides practical space and facilities for artists specialising in sculpture, printmaking and pottery.
- **Law Uk Folk Museum** Converted from restored Hakka village house, complete with furnitre and farming tools, p60.
- **Macau Grand Prix Museum** With winning vehicles from the Macau Grand Prix, plus interactive simulators, p113.
- **Macau Wine Museum** Charting the importance of wine to the Portugese from its earliest roots, p113.
- **Museum of Coastal Defence** An underground battery, telescopes and series of galleries depicting maritime history from the Ming Dynasty to the Japanese occupation, p58.
- **Police Museum** The old Wan Chai Gap Police Station now charts the history of one of the world's oldest forces, p62.
- **Sam Tung Uk Museum** A rare glimpse into the area's former years before the textile industry, p95.
- **Sheung Yiu Folk Museum** An old, 19th-century Hakka village giving a glimpse into rural life, p88.
- **University Museum and Art Gallery University of Hong Kong**, 94 Bonham Rd, Central, **T** 2241 5500 www.hku.hk/hkumag *0930-1800 Mon-Sat, 1330-1730 Sun.* Contains over 1000 Chinese antiquities, and a tea-tasting gallery.

New Territories

Outlying Islands

Macau 107

Ex-Portuguese colony with Chinese and Mediterranean flavours, casinos galore, long leisurely lunches, antique shopping, ruined churches and remote beaches.

See Map 6, page 256, for location of places in this section.

New Territories

Sai Kung Peninsula

Sai Kung is one of Hong Kong's best areas for isolated picturesque scenery, with over 7,500 hectares of open countryside and wonderful views of the water and many walking trails. It is also popular for its beaches and seafood. There are country parks with well-established trails, but with a little effort it is possible to come across dilapidated villages and remote outlying islands that leave the crowds and chaos of Hong Kong far behind. The main fishing village, which has always been a popular expat enclave, makes a suitable base for hiking and camping with a good selection of restaurants and bars, as well as the main transport hub with buses and kaidos (see p28).

▸▸ *See Eating and drinking p149, Shopping p187, Sports p201*

◉ Sights

★ Sai Kung
Sai Kung Country Park Visitor Centre, **T** 2793 7365. *Wed-Mon 0930-1630. Minibus no 1A from Choi Hung Station. Bus no 94 to Pak Tam Chung.* Map 6, p256

This small resort town, also known as Hong Kong's Garden is a relaxing seaside base for some wonderful trekking in the surrounding three country parks. A popular expat enclave, it has many decent bars and restaurants, as well as a good bunch of harbour-front seafood restaurants on Sai Kung Tai Kai St, along which sampans sell fresh fish at around 1700 daily. This area gets even busier during the local seafood festival, part of HKTB's Food Festival. From here, it is possible to hire sampans and kaidos to sail to the outlying islands and beaches from one of the many persuasive ladies; haggling is essential and it helps to have a Cantonese speaker.

New Territories Heritage Hall, has life-size reproductions of boats, part of a Chinese merchant ship, village houses and shops. The **T T Tsui Gallery of Chinese Art** has miniature models of classic Chinese furniture in Ming style made from rosewood. It also has models of how wooden furniture is built without nails – an interesting lesson before visiting Chi Lin Nunnery.

● *On your way to the museum, follow signs from Sha Tin station for Pai Tau Village, one of the only remaining Qing dynasty villages, today just a small street of old houses with large balconies and gardens. The houses are still inhabited and prove to be a far more desirable alternative to the cramped apartment block. At the end of the street is a Wong's Kitchen and Café (see Eating and drinking, p150.)*

Sha Tin Racecourse

Sha Tin. KCR: Racecourse (race days only), **T** 2695 6223. Hong Kong Jockey Club **T** 1817. *Racing season Sep-Jun. Penfold Park (closed Mon and racedays) KCR: Fo Tan.*

Although not possessing the dramatic visual impact of a night race meeting at Happy Valley, the weekend afternoon race meetings at Sha Tin make for good entertainment. Completed in 1978 and built on reclaimed land with the proceeds from night racing at Happy Valley, it is an ultra-modern racetrack which has also landscaped the infield to create **Penfold Park**, one of Hong Kong's largest, which contains a bird sanctuary. The biggest (and richest) races of the year are the Hong Kong Cup, Hong Kong Mile, Hong Kong Vase and Hong Kong Sprint. Entrance costs $10 to the public stand, and tourists staying in Hong Kong for less than 21 days may buy a guest badge for the Member's Stand (bring passport), which are also for sale at the off-course betting branches.

● *On your way to the racecourse, increase your chances of backing a winner by visiting the ancient Che Kung Temple in nearby Tai Wai, where local race-goers flock to offer prayers and seek divine fortune.*

Ten Thousand Buddhas Monastery and Po Fook Ancestral Hall
KCR: Sha Tin. *Daily 0900-1700.*

The stiff climb up more than 400 steps to the monastery (Man Fat Tsz in Cantonese) is well worth it, with a forecourt and nine-storey red-and-gold pagoda filled with miniature Buddhas and shrine images, at the top of which are some wonderful views including Amah Rock. Built in the 1950s, there are around 13,000 golden statues of the Lord Buddha lining the walls of the main prayer hall, each one slightly different from the last. In Chinese, the number 10,000 is used to signify a countless number, thereby indicating many more Buddhas than the actual number in the monastery. There are also statues of animals, gaudy statues of Buddhist gods, fortune tellers who often work in the main hall, and the encased mummified corpse of the temple's founding abbot.

Lower down the hill is the Po Fook Ancestral Hall, built in the 1990s, containing pavilions, a red-trimmed pagoda and landscaped terraces, and dozens of small shrines – the resting place for the ashes and ancestral tablets of thousands of dead souls.

Tai Po

*Deep into the New Territories and west of Tolo Harbour, Tai Po was one of the oldest-known settlements of Hong Kong dating back 4,500 years, first inhabited by fishermen and later an important centre for the pearl fishing trade. After the 17th century it became a market town and home to the Tangs, one of Hong Kong's original clans, but these days it is a growing industrial satellite town. However, it is still of interest especially for its **market**, the beautiful **Man Mo Temple** on Fu Shin St, and as a base to explore the nearby **Plover Cove**.*

Tai Po's attractions are included in a self-guided walk, for which there is audio equipment which can be borrowed from the Hong Kong Tourist Board, Star Ferry Concourse, see p34.

◉ Sights

Tai Po Market
Map 6, p256

As Tai Po has been a market town since the 17th century, its
market provides a tiny remnant of its traditional past in the midst
of modern town planning, although what is officially called the
Temporary Market, has only been in operation relatively recently.
Its original market was controlled by the Tang Clan, who imposed
huge tariffs for ferry rides across the river. In the late 19th century
the Man Clan set up their own market, built Man Mo Temple and a
footbridge over the river. Predominantly on sale these days are
fish, fruit, vegetables, meat and household goods.

Hong Kong Railway Museum
13 Shung Tak St, Tai Po. **T** 2653 3455, www.lcsd.gov.hk *0900-1700;
closed Tue.*

In the old Tai Po Market station, which was built in 1913, this small
museum has old railway carriages to explore, a narrow gauge
engine, photographs of the opening of the Kowloon-Canton
Railway, and coaches dating back to 1911 on the outside tracks.
The building was declared a historical monument in 1984.

Lam Tsuen Wishing Tree and Tin Hau Temple
Lam Tsuen Village. *Map 6, p256*

The Wishing Tree, outside the Tin Hau Temple in Lam Tsuen
village, is an ancient banyan, now garlanded with red and gold
incense papers thanks to the belief that it has the power to grant
wishes. Especially during Lunar New Year, worshippers scribble
their wishes on red paper (having supposed to have prayed all

year), tied to an orange with string. They throw it up to the branches and if it gets caught on the tree, the wish is thought to come true. Next to the tree are women selling the oranges and paper for around $5, which if nothing else at least gives the opportunity to see what a good aim you have. The temple was built around the time of the Emperor Qian Long of the Qing Dynasty and was the largest of its kind in Tai Po. The main hall of the temple is devoted to Tin Hau, while those at either side are for Man (god of literature) and Mo (god of war), which is not uncommon in Hong Kong temples.

● *For a view over Tolo Harbour and the Chinese border, climb the Lookout Tower, a pseudo space-age construction over 32m high, in Tai Po Waterfront Park. Access is between 0900-1800.*

Kadoorie Farm and Botanical Garden

Facing Lam Kam Rd, Tai Po, **T** 2488 1317, www.kfbg.org *0930-1700. Maps are available at the reception centre for $5. Registering on arrival and departure is necessary, and advance booking advisable. Bus no 64K or taxi from Tai Po Market KCR station.*

Set up in the 1950s by the Kadoorie family, initially as an experimental breeding station and to provide thousands of post-Second World War refugees with a means of employment, this hilltop farm covers more than 145 hectares and focuses on education and conservation. It contains walking trails, animal conservatories, a butterfly farm, plants and exotic animals and is especially popular with children, and the Kadoorie Brothers' Memorial Pavilion at the farm's highest point is the perfect spot to enjoy the surrounding expanse of flowers and trees. This, plus another high point at Kwun Yum Shan, is a good 3-4 hour walk away. The insect house is a big hit with kids, containing all manner of creepie-crawlies and no doubt the instigator of many a bed-time story. There is no food available at the farm, so come with a picnic.

Other sights in the New Territories

Fung Ying Seen Koon Temple
Fanling. *KCR: Fanling. Map 6, p256*

This is one of the most interesting temples in Hong Kong, not only for its sheer size and the wonderful example of Taoist design of the orange-tiled double roof dominating the skyline, but also for its 10 ancestral halls. Each one is crammed from floor to ceiling with rows of tiny ancestral tablets to which relatives pray, although the sight of all the photographs of departed souls looking out blankly can have a slightly macabre edge. To lighten up the atmosphere, the huge grounds also contain beautiful sculptures of the Chinese zodiac symbols, a herbal medicine clinic and an orchid terrace. Look out for the Wall of Daode Jing, a huge mural depicting the 72 immortals made from black marble and etched with gold. Sundays and festivals are especially busy, when many visitors come to burn offerings for their dead relatives. ● *On your way to Fung Ying Seen Koon, stop off at **Hu Kun Chung Temple** (on the other side of Pak Wo Rd), interesting if only to compare the two. This Buddhist temple, completed in 1980 and the epitome of tranquility, has an old people's home in its grounds.*

Mai Po Marshes
Mai Po Nature Reserve **T** 2471 6306, maipo@wwf.org.hk Tours **T** 2366 5266; permits **T** 2526 4473. *Tours Tue, Thu and Sun (Oct-Apr). Map 6, p256*

Rated as one of China's seven most important wetlands, also known as Ramsar sites, and close to its border, this is a haven for thousands of birds and reptiles and an important point on the migration route. It is known to contain 15 endangered waterbird species, especially black-faced spoonbill, Saunder's gull and Dalmatian pelican, and over 20 new species of invertebrates have been found. In 2001, it was estimated that 252 spoonbills came for the winter before heading back to Korea, and the marshes are thought to contain around 25% of its world's population. The wetlands are a stopover for tens of thousands of birds along the East Asia-Australasian flyway, which is why 80% of the population is migratory. The marshes are also home to otters, butterflies and leopard cats.

Paths and trails lead to ponds, reed beds, mangroves and mudflats and at the centre of the marshes is the Mai Po Nature Reserve with bird-watching platforms, *best time to visit Oct-May*. The World Wildlife Fund for Nature, which plays a large role in running the reserve, organizes tours including a visit to the 3-storey tower hide with views of the entire marshes, every Tuesday, Thursday and Sunday, *Oct-Apr*, lasting around 5 hours. It also offers permits to foreign tourists, on a first-come-first-served basis.

⬤ *The term 'Ramsar' comes from the town Ramsar in Iran, host of a convention for conserving the world's most important wetlands. Of the 118 countries now part of Ramsar, Hong Kong joined in 1979. It now has an international obligation to protect its valuable wetlands including Mai Po Marshes, one of the seven Ramsar sites in China.*

Sam Tung Uk Museum
2 Kwu Uk Lane, Tsuen Wan, **T** 2411 2001, stum@lcsd.gov.hk
0900-1700; closed Tue and some public holidays.   Map 6, p256

This historic Hakka walled village was built by the Chan Clan in 1786, and declared a monument in 1981. It underwent extensive restoration before being opened to the public, and won a Pacific Heritage Award from the Pacific Asia Tourist Association in 1990. Tseun Wan went through tremendous changes long before other areas in the New Territories, mainly because of relocating textile manufacturers from Shanghai, which meant that factories replaced farmland. Sam Tung Uk is one of the last reminders of its previous existence, after the remaining villages had to be relocated when Tseun Wan MTR station was built.

Lantau Link Viewing Platform
Tsing Ye. *Minibus no 308M from Tsing Ye MTR. Viewing Platform: 0700-2230 Sun-Fri, 0700-0130 Sat and public holidays. Visitors' Centre: 1000-1700 Mon-Fri, 1000-1830 Sat, Sun and public holidays.*

Tsing Ma Bridge, the world's longest road-and-rail suspension bridge at 2.2 km, is also the venue of the viewing platform and visitors' centre. The platform overlooks Lantau Link and Tsing Ma, Kap Shui Mun and Ting Kau Bridges. The visitors' centre also has models and photos of the link, and a cross-section of the main suspension cable.

Outlying Islands

Lantau

*Twice the size of Hong Kong Island, yet home to just 25,000 people, Lantau has a huge variety of places to visit. The main attractions are the **Big Buddha**, hikes in the **country parks**, **beaches** and **traditional villages**. With a wide choice of good value hotels and restaurants, plus 24-hour transport to Hong Kong and Kowloon, and convenient for the airport, it's worth considering using Lantau as a base and making day trips to other parts of the territory. For the price of a tiny room in traffic and pollution on Hong Kong Island, you can stay in a peaceful, large room overlooking the beach.*

▸▸ *See Sleeping p127, Eating and drinking p150, Bars and clubs p164*

 Sights

Big Buddha and Po Lin Monastery
Ngong Ping, Lantau, **T** 2985 5248. *1000-1730. Meals at Po Lin: 1130-1630, $60. Po Lin exhibitions 1000-1600. Map 6, p256*

The first sighting of one of Hong Kong's biggest (literally) attractions is imposing: from the bus winding its way to the Po Lin Monastery, the back of the Buddha can be seen over the hills. Set amid spectacular mountain scenery, the monastery, which was built in 1924, shares Ngong Ping Plateau with the famous Big Buddha. From the bottom of the 268 wide, flag-lined steps leading up to the bronze statue, the size of the largest outdoor seated Buddha in the world (Hong Kong loves its superlatives) really sinks in, even more so when you're standing directly underneath its hand and looking up. Completed in 1989, inaugurated in 1993, and weighing in at 202 tonnes and standing at 26 metres, it attracts bus-loads of tourists daily, especially on Sundays. Wrap up warm because the weather can be bitterly cold and windy at the top.

Once at the top, there is a fantastic view of the rolling green of Lantau (if there is no haze) and several statues along the balcony. An interesting exhibition inside the base explains how the statue was built in Nanjing in China then transported here in pieces, and huge paintings illustrate the story of Buddhism. This is free, although the exhibition hall upstairs is only open to those who have purchased (from the kiosk at the bottom of the steps) a $60 meal voucher for the monastery.

There are mixed feelings about the **restaurant** inside Po Lin Monastery, which is accessible across the car park and down the path. The pure vegetarian set meal is wholesome and filling, although the service is surly. More pleasant dining experiences are available at the adjacent self-service café and **Tea Garden Restaurant** (see p151), a 10-minute walk from the car park.

Within the monastery there is an **Exhibition of Secret Documents of Buddhist Activity** in Qing Palace, covering two halls. The main temple has a bright red ceiling garishly adorned with

! The computer-controlled bell inside the Buddha rings 108 times a day, to symbolize the escape of the so-called 108 troubles of mankind.

paintings and figures and outside are huge stone pillars carved with dragons. The iron pots outside contain 10-foot high incense sticks, burning heavily. You can buy them from adjacent stalls.

● *More ambitious hikers can climb nearby Lantau Peak which, at 934m, is Hong Kong's second highest peak. The best map is in the South China Morning Post trekking guide, see p238.*

★ Tai O
Map 6, p256

Because of its proximity to mainland China, Tai O used to be notorious for its piracy and even today it is implied that certain goods get 'delivered' by fishing boat. Once the centre of the salt trade to China, the oldest of the few remaining fishing villages in Hong Kong, has changed over the years. A third of the **stilt houses**, for which the village is famed, were mysteriously burned down in July 2000. The Government built characterless concrete blocks to rehouse people but many refused, preferring to rebuild their own houses.

The aluminium stilt houses are like silver boxes and said to originate from the Tanka people, the first fishermen of Hong Kong, who felt unsafe on land. Most are two storeys, with brightly painted window frames propped up with wood, and terraces brimming with pots of plants and household clutter. Between the houses are narrow wooden pedestrian ramps over the creek, making it possible to wander between the rows.

From the bus station, *bus no 1 from Mui Wo*, and taxi rank, there is a bamboo scaffold for **Chinese Opera** and down this tiny street are a couple of good cheap restaurants, rather like dining in someone's kitchen (see p151). Back into the centre of the village, there is a pleasant walk down **Wing On Street** amidst shops selling dried salted fish and trays of egg yolks drying in the sun. Sundays are busier, when you can hear the clattering of mahjong tiles emerging from apartments.

Walking on water
The aluminium stilt houses in the traditional fishing village of Tai O are the last of a dying breed.

▶ All change in Tai O?

Government plans to give Tai O a facelift, costing nearly $300m, were met with strong opposition from some of the locals. Legislators approved the funding and plans include a new boat anchorage to provide a sheltered basin for fishing vessels, a promenade and steps covering an area of four hectares, all to be completed by August 2005. To compensate for the loss of huge areas of mangroves during construction of the new airport, seven hectares have been put aside for replanting. The Tai O Rural Committee hopes that the village can be developed into a true fishing port which would boost its economy thanks to an estimated 150,000 extra tourists a year. But its opponents are worried that the project will destroy the village's tranquillity, original characteristics, heritage and scenery, and are concerned that the government is gearing everything for mass tourism. The arguments for job creation and improvement of the local economy are certainly valid, but it will be a shame if Tai O is turned into a fishing theme park.

A new, manually operated **drawbridge** spans the narrow creek that divides the town, replacing the old-fashioned rope-drawn "ferry" operated by the village old dears for over 86 years. The other side has an HSBC on Kat Hing St. On the first alleyway to the right, Yun Tan lives like a hermit in his secluded shop and is thought to be the only traditional **mask maker** in Hong Kong, carving heroes and gods out of wood.

Off Kat Hing Street is the village square containing **Kwan Tai Temple** and the marriage registry office. Tai O **Market Street** has another collection of seafood restaurants, packed at weekends. Out towards **Po Chue Tam** sampans chug around the old stilt houses for a closer look inside a fast-disappearing way of life.

Cheung Sha

No 4 bus from Mui Wo. It is also possible to get on the Airport Express, or buses going to Tai O or Ngong Ping which all go in the same direction, although you will probably have to pay the full journey fare.
Map 6, p256

One of Hong Kong's cleanest and most beautiful beaches, Cheung Sha is relatively isolated. From the bus stop for Cheung Sha Lower village, walk down the steep path leading to a tiny car park and gift shop. Stock up on food for a picnic at the supermarkets at Mui Wo, or eat at **The Stoep** or **Kung Shing Restaurant** (see p151). There are changing facilities and showers at the far end of the beach, near to a small shop renting out umbrellas and mats. The water is clean and waves attract surfers, and junk trips often stop off on the beach for a meal. Past the changing rooms is a new Chinese pavilion on the hill, to where it is possible to walk – worth it for the great views. The beach gets crowded during fine weekends and is blissfully isolated during the week.

Mui Wo

Map 6, p256

The main hub of this half of Lantau is the location of the ferry pier, buses and taxis, banks, bars, shops and restaurants. Turn right from the ferry pier and a little further on is the cooked food market, which has a great selection of little Chinese and seafood restaurants offering semi-alfresco dining, the best of which is **Yee Hen** (see p152). Walk up Ngan Kwong Road, past the hospital post office, and across the bridge near the market is a new block containing an interesting **antique shop** (see p189). Continue past the children's playground to the **old village** of Mui Wo, then wander down Mui Wo Rural Committee Road which has a real village atmosphere and plenty of good cheap restaurants. This is one of the most interesting areas of the island – a genuine example of rural village life. There are footpaths leading to the beach which, although a vast white expanse, is not the best area for bathing, and is also the location of several hotels and guest houses.

Tung Chung

Direct bus from Mui Wo, Po Lin Monastery and Discovery Bay, on the MTR line and there are half-hourly ferries to Tuen Mun. The fort (0900-1600) is a 25-min walk from Tung Chung terminus. MTR: Tung Chung. Buses from Mui Wo and Discovery Bay. Map 6, p256

Since the completion of the new airport nearby, Tung Chung has transformed itself from an ancient fishing village into a new town, and will soon be one of the largest satellite towns in Hong Kong. Its shopping mall is linked to the MTR station and contains several restaurants, a cinema, and decent shopping which even attracts Discovery Bay residents with regular direct buses between the two.

Old Tung Chung is interesting and the harbourside Qing dynasty **fort**, built in 1817 to attempt to suppress the opium trade from Guangzhou, is today a local school and government building with six cannons along the ramparts as a reminder of its former glory. **Hau Wong Temple** is a little-known place of interest, containing a bell from the Qianlong dynasty which suggests the temple dates back to 1765, and ceramic decorations produced in the famous kiln of Shiwan during the reign of Xuantong.

Discovery Bay

Map 6, p256

There is little reason to stop by in Discovery Bay as a visitor; a huge concrete housing estate for wealthy expats and their families. But there is a lovely walk from Mui Wo to Discovery Bay, past the **Trappist Monastery** which was founded by immigrants from mainland China and operated as a dairy until recently. From Discovery Bay there are regular fast ferries to Central.

Lamma

With a long-standing reputation as a hippie haven, Lamma has become built up over the years and now resembles a crowded holiday resort with an ugly sprawl of concrete houses – a far cry from the small agricultural and fishing village of a few decades ago. Still popular with expats attracted by low rent, it is the closest inhabited island to Hong Kong and an easy day out with regular fast ferries from Central ferry pier. Yung Shue Wan, the village closest to the main ferry pier, has many restaurants, cafés and shops, but with a little effort and a map there are lovely walks and quiet villages to explore.

▸▸ *See Sleeping p129 and Eating and drinking p152*

See Sleeping p129 and Eating and drinking p152

Walk from Yung Shue Wan to Sok Kwu Wan
1 hr, suitable for children.   Map 6, p256

At the end of the Main Street, chock-full of restaurants and shops, a charming little temple, lacking the usual temple opulence, is guarded by two stone lions. The path from here to the tiny **Hung Shing Ye beach** takes around half an hour, through plantations of ginger lily and banana trees and a couple of unnamed cafés. Overlooking the tiny beach, usually packed on Sundays, is the **Concerto Inn** (see p152) which serves decent food on the terrace, although the power station looming in front mars the view. From the beach, the path climbs gently to the **Chinese pavilion**, with good views over Lamma, Cheung Chau and Lantau. From here, **Sok Kwu Wan beach** is well signposted and has good seafood restaurants, although the water is not great for swimming.

Other walks and beaches
Map 6, p256

The marked trail from **Sok Kwu Wan** to **Shan Tei Tong** (Mount Stenhouse) at 353 m is a tough climb that gets progressively easier. Another alternative from Yung Shue Wan is to turn off to the right just before reaching Sok Kwu Wan and walk to **Lo So Shing**, on the western side of the narrow strip of land in the middle of Lamma, which is a much better beach (with a lifeguard during summer). During the Tang Dynasty (seventh-10th century) it was the centre of the local industry, baking seashells to make lime, and there are still two kilns in front of the school and seven beside the nearby beach. At the south of the island is **Sham Wan**, also known as Turtle Beach. It is the only place on Lamma where green turtles are nesting and laying eggs. It is now protected by a marine park and prevents people entering during the season and stealing the eggs.

Another way of reaching Hong Kong island is a ferry to Aberdeen, either from the northernmost village of **Pak Kok**, or from **Mo Tat Wan** on the east.

★ Cheung Chau

*Cheng Chau, literally meaning "long island" and shaped like a dumb-bell, is just 2.4 km square and the most densely populated of the outlying islands. The busy harbourside promenade, the **Praya**, is lined with shops and restaurants, although the best dining is in the popular **seafood restaurants**, the island's biggest attraction for Hong Kong residents. No cars are allowed and the only motorized vehicles permitted are tiny ambulances and fire engines. Dozens of wooden junk boats are moored in the harbour, home to fishing families who maintain a traditional lifestyle, aided by the latest modern technology.*

Cheung Chau's most famous resident is Lee Lai Shan, better known as San San, Hong Kong's first ever Olympic gold medallist, winning it for windsurfing during the 1996 Atlanta games. Her success has inspired a huge interest in watersports and Tung Wan Beach, where she trained as a schoolgirl, has a windsurfing centre and equipment for hire, p208.

▶ Bun Festival

Without doubt, the island's busiest time of the year and one of Hong Kong's most colourful festivals, the Bun Festival is a huge carnival specific to Cheung Chau. During the 18th century, the island was devastated by a plague and infiltrated by pirates who massacred the locals. Fishermen brought an image of the god Pak Tai to the island to try and placate the ghosts of the murdered victims by parading it around the lanes. The evil spirits were driven away and hence the island celebrates the annual four-day thanksgiving festival, around April or May. Visitors flock here to see the festivities, most famously the enormous towers of buns built in front of the Pak Tai temple, which people previously tried to climb to reach the highest buns for good luck, until an accident causing many injuries ended the fun. Ornately costumed children are 'mounted' on rods and carried above the crowds, as though floating.

Pak Tai Temple
A 5-min walk along San Hing St, turning left out of the ferry pier.
Map 6, p256

Built in 1783, here is a temple dedicated to Pak Tai, Taoist god of the sea and protector of fishermen or, more sternly put, the "Supreme Emperor of the Dark Heaven". His power is symbolized by the serpent and tortoise on the ground, and there are two statues of generals at his altar, Thousand Miles Eye and Favourable Wind Ear, who are said to see and hear any distance. Set in its own little courtyard with ceramic figures on the roof ridges and stone lions, it was completely repainted in 1989 and is now gloriously colourful. Some of its historical relics date back 800 years, including a Sung Dynasty sword and an antique sedan chair. The temple is the centre of festivities for the Bun Festival (see above).

Tung Wan Beach
Map 6, p256

On the eastern side of the narrow strip of land and a 15-minute walk from the pier, this popular beach is home to the island's largest hotel, the **Warwick** (see p130). At the base of the hotel are 3000-year-old Bronze Age rock carvings encased in glass. It is also home to the famous **Cheung Chau Windsurfing Centre** (see p208), a mecca for local watersports enthusiasts.

Other islands

Peng Chau
Map 6, p256

Just one-third of the size of Cheung Chau, Peng Chau is linked to Central and Cheung Chau by an inter-island ferry, and is a scaled-down model of the others with many of the traditional ways of life still remaining. Although not really interesting enough to merit a full day out, it makes a pleasant excursion wandering around the **fishing harbour**, the 200-year-old **Tin Hau temple**, the morning **fish market** and the little cottage industry of **hand-painted porcelain**. There is a well-marked family trail around the island, and fresh seafood can be bought at the old pier and then taken to local restaurants for cooking. There is a kaido, a tiny ferry, across to the peaceful Trappist Monastery on Lantau and ferries to Central and Mui Wo.

Po Toi Islands
Map 6, p256

The picturesque Po Toi Islands lie off the southeast of Hong Kong Island, accessible via Aberdeen or Stanley, and are one of the most remote and unspoilt areas of Hong Kong. **Po Toi**, the largest, and where the ferries dock, is a rugged outcrop which is great for rough hill trails and isolated walking along the granite headland above the cliffs, and it also has wonderful seafood and an interesting **Tin Hau temple**. There are ancient rock carvings and the occasional sighting of white-bellied sea eagles and turtles.

It is also possible to visit other tiny islands like **Tap Mun**, accessible via Sai Kung or Tolo Harbour, which is an old-fashioned fishing community. **Tung Lung**, which has an interesting old fort, is accessible by keido on weekends and public holidays or by two ferries from Sai Wan Ho Ferry Pier.

Macau

*The Macau Special Administrative Region (SAR), which is part of mainland China, comprises a peninsula and two islands in the Pearl River Delta. Most of its attractions, entertainment and hotels are in Macau itself. **Taipa** and **Coloane islands**, linked by bridges and causeway and accessible by taxi or bus, are known for their old villages, beaches and country walks. While most of the museums are not a patch on those in Hong Kong, Macau's beauty lies in its churches, fortresses, temples and cobbled squares, as well as the Mediterranean feel of its architecture and street life. Taipa's most interesting areas are the shophouses and narrow streets around its historical old village and the newly restored elegant mansions along its waterfront. Coloane is most popular with those who truly want to escape crowds and traffic and has the best beaches and walks.*

▸▸ *See Sleeping p130, Eating and drinking p153, Bars and clubs p165*

Senate Square
Holy House of Mercy and Museum, Largo do Senado. *1000-1300 and 1500-1730, closed Sun. MOP5, children free.*

This attractive square has distinctive wave-patterned mosaic cobblestones, extending via Sao Domingo's church and Sao

Paulo. Surrounded by pastel-coloured traditional buildings in arcade style, it's the city's centrepiece for musical and cultural events and a great people-watching venue with benches, a fountain, cafés and the start of a huge pedestrianized street lined with shops. Dominating the square is the 16th-century **Leal Senado**, the former Senate's house and now the Civic and Municipal Affairs Bureau, and a wonderful example of neoclassical Portuguese architecture. Nearby are the **GPO**, the helpful **Macau Tourist Office** and the **Holy House of Mercy and Museum**, containing oil paintings, ancient manuscripts, religious artefacts and ivory statues along with Chinese, Japanese and European porcelain pieces.

Avenida de Almeida Ribeiro and Rua da Felicidade

These are two of Macau's most interesting streets: Ribeiro runs from Largo do Senado to the old docks, a lively main road with banks and shophouses selling jewellery (gold is cheaper here than in Hong Kong), food, wine and clothes. At the western end are the shabby old docks, fish hanging on the railings to dry, without the graceful architecture, but nonetheless full of character. Parallel to Ribeiro is Rue da Felicidade, one-time red-light area (appropriately translating as 'Happiness Street'), with a great collection of restaurants, bakeries selling Macanese cakes, dried squares of pressed beef, wild boar and pigeon and cheap guesthouses. The street had facelift a recently – the small shophouses were whitewashed and their window shutters painted bright red.

Ruins of St Paul's Church and Museum of Sacred Art
Rua de Sao Paulo.

Macau's most striking symbol, dramatically poised at the top of a grand staircase, is all that remains of the Jesuit church built in the early 17th century, and it is easy to imagine why it was once described as the greatest church east of Rome. The façade has intricate carvings depicting an angel carrying a cross, the sea star guiding the church, saints, the Immaculate Conception and the Holy Spirit. When the Jesuits were expelled, the church, along with the adjacent Mater Dei College, fell into disrepair and was destroyed by fire in 1835. Extensive excavations in the 1990s revealed the old crypt containing the bones of Vietnamese and Japanese martyrs, now sensitively displayed, while religious paintings, sculptures and the remains of the college founder are on view in Museum of Sacred Art, behind.

Cultural Club

390-396 Av de Almeida Ribeiro, **T** 921 811, www.culturalclub.net *1030-2100.*

The old Tak Seng pawnshop has recently been converted into a museum and shop, spread over three floors with beautiful dark wooden floorboards and balcony, selling traditional arts and crafts. The highlight is the **Water Tea House** (2/F), a traditional and tranquil tearoom, where tea is prepared at your table with all the appropriate ceremony and utensils. The elaborate process is fascinating, beginning with your waitress snipping each foil-wrapped portion of tea-leaves, heating up each cup, pouring it into the 'smelling cup', cleaning the leaves by discarding the first lot of boiling water, then pouring into the drinking cup. A portion of tea makes around 20 cups, each one a little larger than a thimble.

● *Around the corner from the Cultural Club is Rua de Camilo Pessanha, a grubby street packed full of unusual shops selling Chinese medicine, paper "money" to burn for loved ones, dai pai dongs, barbers and mahjong sets.*

Museum of Macau and Sao Paulo Monte Fort

112 Praceta do Museu de Macau, **T** 357 911,
www.macaumuseum.gov.mo *1000-1800, closed Mon. MOP15,
MOP8 children under 11. Free on 15th day of each month.*

The fort was built by the Jesuits in 1626 as part of the Sao Paulo
church, to defend the city against Dutch fleets. It was used as the
residence of governor Mascarenhas until 1749, then fell into
disrepair until destroyed by fire. Now only the cannons, (used only
once – to destroy the Dutch in 1622), ramparts and Meteorological
Department remain, with a friendly little café-bar at the top. There
are wonderful views over the peninsula and mainland China.

The new museum occupies the fort's foundations and platform,
spread over three floors: the first floor is devoted to Macau's early
history and birth as a commercial port. The second depicts popular
arts and tradition with life-size models of street hawkers, festivals
and house interiors, while the top floor deals with urban
development and contemporary Macau.

⬤ *Look out for the booklet of the Macau Cricket Fight
Association, and the tombs and coffins made from glass, wood or
marble in which champion fighting crickets would be sent to their
final resting place.*

Guia Fort and Lighthouse

Estrada de Cacilhas. *0900-1730. Cable car: 0730-1830. MOP3
(single), MOP5 (return).*

Built in 1638 at the highest point of the city by Antonio Ribeiro,
Captain of Artillery, the fort was designed to defend the border
with China but in time became more relevant as an observation
post. With barracks, water cistern and ammunition stores, its
most prominent feature is the oldest lighthouse on the China
coast, built in 1865, whose light can be seen for 20 miles on a
clear day. The adjacent early-17th-century chapel has antique

pictures, an image of the Virgin Mary, a simple baroque altar, and paintings dating back to 1622 which were only rediscovered during restoration in 1996. From Flora Garden, adjacent to the fort, is the world's shortest cable car whose 80-second journey descends to street level.

★ Greyhound Racing at the Canindrome

Av Do Almirante Lacerda, **T** 221 199, www.macaudog.com
2000-2230 (Tue, Thu, Sat and Sun). MOP10 (refundable on first bet).

The only dog track in Asia makes for a hugely entertaining night out, attracting thousands of punters each week. From the main enclosure, punters can get close enough to the track to see the fear in the rabbit's eyes. The huge, computerized tote board displays the ever-mounting totals for win, place, quinella and trifecta bets; confusing to the novice but friendly public relations staff near the betting booths will help fill out your betting card. For MOP30, refundable against refreshments, indoor gallery seats are available and waiters bring food and drink to your table, although limited to the usual Chinese fare of lungs, ears and feet, washed down with beer. If you need a desperate fix between races, there are slot machines to pass the time.

🔘 *For MOP10 you can have your photo taken with the "beautiful bitch" Cheeky Cat (as described by the Canindrome Club), a charming white-and-fawn winner of 18 races before retiring in 1999. She now reclines regally in a trackside tent and will happily pose with punters while a Club photographer takes your souvenir picture.*

! There has been trouble at the tracks since 2002: Hong Kong ruled that their citizens would no longer be permitted use of off-course betting centres in Hong Kong to gamble on the dogs or horses in Macau, or place bets over the phone. Macau is not happy – the move putting both the Canindrome and Jockey Club in, as one official described, a "critical position".

Macau Tower

Largo da Torre de Macau, **T** 933 339, www.macautower.com.mo
*1000-2100. Carousel Kiosk barbecue 1200-1430, MOP50; and
1830-2200, MOP98.*

Looming 338 m over the Pearl River Delta, Macau Tower opened in
2001 and is the 10th tallest free-standing tower in the world. It offers
entertainment, exhibitions, shopping and eating. Not for the faint-
hearted, its main attractions include the glass-floored observation
deck, to peer between your feet 58 floors down onto the city. The
Skywalk involves walking around the outside of the tower wearing a
safety harness, just the metal ridge separating you from the ground.
For a view without an adrenaline rush, the **360° Café** is a revolving
Chinese restaurant, *1200-1500 and 1830-2300;* **180° Lounge** offers a
semi-panorama with drinks and snacks, *1200-0100,* with weekend
barbecues at the outdoor Carousel Kiosk back on ground level.

Old Protestant Cemetery and Casa Garden

Praca Luis de Camoes

The wilderness-like Casa Garden was once the headquarters of the
British East Indian Company and, after it left in 1835, a grotto was
built for Luis de Camoes, the famous Portuguese soldier-poet. The
beautiful, neoclassical house is now the office of the Fundação
Oriente, a Macau cultural foundation. The adjacent early-19th-
century cemetery contains the graves of Protestant residents, sailors
and visitors, plus a motley crew of opium traders, missionaries, and
some of the crew of Commodore Perry's fleet that opened up Japan.

A-Ma Temple

Barra Point

Macau's name is derived from A-Ma-Gau, or place of A-Ma, so this
temple overlooking the harbour and dedicated to A-Ma, goddess

of fishermen, is the most important in Macau. A 16th-century legend tells of a poor girl looking for a ride to Canton, refused by wealthy junk owners but taken on board by a fisherman. None of them survived a strong storm, but she reappeared as a goddess and a temple was built on the same spot, consisting of player halls, pavilions and courtyards.

Macau Grand Prix Museum

Tourism Activity Centre, Rua Luis Gonzaga Gomes, **T** 7984 108. *1000-1800; closed Tue. MOP10, MOP5 children 11-18. MOP20 with Wine Museum.*

A must for anyone with dreams of being a racing driver: including some of the cars and bikes that have won the Macau Grand Prix, videos and memorabilia of great drivers and interactive simulators.

Macau Wine Museum

Tourism Activity Centre, Rua Luis Gonzaga Gomes, **T** 7984 188. *1000-1800; closed Tue. MOP10, MOP5 children 11-18. MOP20 with Grand Prix Museum.*

With a free taste of wine or port to get you in the mood, the museum goes back to the very earliest era of wine making, and its importance in Portuguese culture. Exhibiting maps, photos, models of equipment and a cellar, there are explanations of the different regions and their grapes, with more than 1,000 different brands on display. If inspired, there is a shop selling a (smaller) range of bottles.

Kun lam Temple

Av do Coronel Mesquita

Macau's largest temple, and one of the wealthiest, is dedicated to the Buddhist goddess of Mercy and was founded in the 13th century. It has a huge entrance gate, whose roofs are clustered with porcelain figures, and the richly decorated halls, separated by courtyards, are devoted to the Precious Buddha, the Buddha of Longevity, and Kun Iam. The terraced temple gardens have interesting historical items, including the stone table where the USA and China signed their first commercial treaty in 1844.

Maritime Museum

T 307 161, www.museumaritimo.gov.mo *1000-1730; closed Tue. MOP10, MOP5 children.*

Located on the site where the first Chinese fishermen and Portuguese traders landed, and opposite A-Ma temple, the museum has sail-shaped walls and portholed-style windows, and is dedicated to the seafaring history of the territory. Outside are reproductions of a Chinese junk, Portuguese lorcha and a dragon boat, while inside there are working sampans, trade-route maps and a fisherman's house, plus a gallery with four aquariums.

Chinese Junk Tours

Pier 1, opp Maritime Museum, **T** 595 481. *Departures at 1030, 1130, 1400, 1500, 1530, 1630 and 1700. MOP12, children free under 12.*

A relaxing half-hour junk ride either along the inner or outer harbour, with commentary about people living on the water.

Old Taipa village

The old village of Taipa is a small, historical area containing shophouses typical of South China which combine beautifully with Mediterranean-style street lamps, hanging baskets and courtyards. Renovated in 1999, the house exteriors and alleyways look European but on closer inspection reveal typical Chinese life. The best time to explore is during the **Sunday Market**, where tiny stalls around the **Largo dos Bombeiros** and **Rua do Regedor**

East meets west
A Mediterranean flavour to the old village of Taipa, Macau

sell cheap household goods, toys, interesting souvenirs and great local snacks. The lively **Rua do Cinha**, also know as Food Street, has the pleasant aroma from many shops baking traditional Macanese biscuits and tiny parcels of curried meat in thin pancakes. On its corner with Rua do Clerigos, a large map on the wall explains the basic history and suggested sightseeing walks, and **Largo Maia de Magalhaes** is a charming old square whose small surrounding streets beg to be explored.

Avenida da Praia Residences
Av da Praia, Taipa. *1000-1800; closed Mon.*

These five elegant white-and-apple green mansions dating back to 1921 and sitting along the old praia waterfront lined with ancient banyan trees, originally belonged to public workers. The first to be converted into a museum in 1990, and the most interesting, is the **Taipa House Museum**.

Hac-Sa and Cheoc Van Beaches
Coloane. *Hac-Sa pool and sport centre: 0800-2100, 0800-2300 (Sun). Cheoc Van swimming pool: 0800-2100; 0800-2400 (Sun). MOP 10, MOP5 children.*

These two beaches have fine, smooth sand and warm water from the Pearl River, and although the water is clean the beach appears dirty because of the silt. Both have restaurants near by, and Hac-Sa (which means Black Sand) has barbecue pits and a good park with a swimming pool and sports facilities. Near Cheoc Van beach is a huge swimming pool with good facilities.

Steep Hong Kong rents mean that space is at a premium, so you generally don't get much for your money although there are endless choices. Hotels range from opulent harbour view suites in Central, to a cheap bed in a cupboard-sized room in Chungking Mansions, with many in between. As a general rule of thumb, most of the cheapest rooms are around **Nathan Road** between Tsim Sha Tsui and Mongkok, still accessible to shopping and eating areas by a short bus ride. The best area for nightlife is between Central and Wan Chai, and most of the top hotels are near the waterfront in Tsim Sha Tsui and Central offering great luxury, at a price. Most mid-range hotels favoured by tour groups and business travellers lack style and individuality, but are functional and well-located. Most of the top and mid-range hotels offer huge discounts throughout the year, often more than 50% off, either directly through the hotel, booking agents or websites, so check out all options if booking in advance. Prices go up and availability down during Chinese New Year, October and the huge Guangzhou fair in April, and Macau hotel prices leap at weekends.

$ Sleeping codes

Price

L	$2500 and over	D	$1000-600
A	$2500-2000	E	$600-400
B	$2000-1500	F	$400-250
C	$1500-1000	G	$250 and under

Prices listed are published rates for low season weekdays (Sun-Thu), standard double with bathroom, exclusive of 13% tax, without breakfast.

Hong Kong Hotels Association, Buffer Halls A & B, Passenger Terminal Building, Hong Kong International Airport, Lantau, **T** 2383 8380 (Hall A), 2769 8822 (Hall B), hrc@hkha.org *0600-2400*. Booking counter after customs. It can usually give decent discounts on rooms, especially mid-range hotels in low season.

Central and Sheung Wan

D Garden View International House, 1 Macdonnell Rd, Central, **T** 2877 3737, **F** 2845 6263, www.ywca.org.hk *MTR: Central. Map 1, D3, p247* A great-value hotel in a prime spot in Central, next to the Peak Tram station and Botanical Garden, and away from the noisy, busy streets. The 130 rooms are pretty spacious, and there is a café on the ground floor, outdoor swimming pool and health centre. Rooms usually available for up to 50% discount, outside peak season.

Admiralty and Wan Chai

C Harbour View International House, 4 Harbour Rd, Wan Chai, **T** 2802 0111, **F** 2802 9063, www.harbour.ymca.org.hk *Map 3, D6, p250* Affiliated to the Chinese YMCA, this is a good quality friendly hotel with 320 small rooms and all but the cheapest rooms have a harbour view. Rooms with TV, kettle, IDD, and tiny bathroom and a restaurant open till 2300. Adjacent to the Arts Centre, it is handily placed for public transport. Promotional rates from $550.

C Hotel New Harbour, 41-49 Hennessy Rd, Wan Chai, **T** 2861 1166, **F** 2865 6111, www.hotelnewharbour.com *Map 3, F6, p250* In the heart of noisy Wan Chai, this unremarkable hotel is popular with Chinese tour groups and has adequate, although relatively small rooms for the price. Standard rooms (the cheapest) are on the 2nd floor, and there are restaurants serving Asian cuisine. Discounts of up to 40% are sometimes available.

D The Wesley, 22 Hennessy Rd, Wan Chai, **T** 2866 6688, **F** 2866 6633, www.grandhotel.com.hk/wesley *Map 3, F5, p250* The 251 no-nonsense pastel-clad rooms attract business travellers, with IDD, cable TV and minibar, but are adequate and reasonable value in the heart of Wan Chai, 5 mins' walk from Pacific Place. There is a Chinese restaurant, and furnished apartments and long-stay packages. Promotions can lower the prices to $400.

D The Wharney Hotel, 57-73 Lockhart Rd, Wan Chai, **T** 2861 1000, **F** 2529 5133, www.wharney.com *Map 3, F7, p251* Uninspiring rooms (361 in total), with decent facilities, such as business centre, gym, pool and Cantonese restaurant. It is handily

Sleeping

located minutes away from the Convention and Exhibition Centre, MTR and Star Ferry to Kowloon. Promotional rates from $600.

Causeway Bay and Happy Valley

E Emperor Hotel, 1 Wang Tak St, Happy Valley, **T** 28933 3693, **F** 2834 6700, www.emperorhotel.com.hk *MTR: Causeway Bay/Happy Valley tram. Map 1, D4, p247* The location is one of its main attractions, adjacent to a quiet residential area near the Happy Valley racetrack. Built in the style of a European deluxe hotel with a grand foyer, the 150 rooms are elegant and comfortable, with cable TV, IDD, internet connection and kettle. Coffee shop and Chinese restaurant also. Great offers bring prices down to $450.

F Hwa Seng Guesthouse, Block B1 5/F Great George Building, 27 Paterson St, Causeway Bay, **T** 2895 6859, **F** 2838 7052, www.guesthouse.com.hk *MTR: Causeway Bay. Map 4, D6, p252* Small, clean rooms, some of which have bathrooms, but the beauty is the location, in the heart of Causeway Bay. Also has very cramped 3- and 4-bedded rooms, but the doubles are fine.

Tsim Sha Tsui

L Peninsula Hotel, Salisbury Rd, **T** 2920 2888, www.peninsula.com *MTR: Tsim Sha Tsui. Map 5, K4, p255 See also page 69* A jazz band plays nightly in the foyer of the grande dame of Hong Kong's hotels. Celebrating its 75th anniversary in 2003, its 300 rooms are huge with ornate carpets, black marble and gold bathrooms (with TV inside). There's also a pool and spa, the renowned restaurant Felix (see p146). Optional extras include Rolls Royce and helicopter transfer for airport and sightseeing. Rooms in low season from $2400.

A Holiday Inn Golden Mile, 50 Nathan Rd, Tsim Sha Tsui, **T** 2369 3111, **F** 2369 8016, www.goldenmile.com *MTR: Tsim Sha*

Tsui. Map 5, I4, p255 A grand, ornate hotel popular with Indian and Japanese tourists, but you really can't get much closer to the noise of Nathan Road. The rooms are big, especially the beds with two double beds in a twin room, and are neatly furnished with the usual facilities, plus voicemail and personal fax machine. There is a rooftop pool, health club, business centre and five restaurants with Asian and western cuisine, plus Hari's bar with live music and good happy hours. Off season prices start at $1,000.

A Marco Polo Hong Kong Hotel, Harbour City, Tsim Sha Tsui, **T** 2113 0088, **F** 2113 0011, www.marcopolohotels.com *MTR: Tsim Sha Tsui. Map 5, J2, p255* One of three five-star hotels of the same group, adjacent to Star Ferry pier and away from the noise of Nathan Rd. The plush 665 rooms have desks, IDD phone with voicemail, cable TV and minibar, and facilities include a business centre, heated outdoor pool and a good range of restaurants. Big discounts available off-season, with rooms from $1000.

C Hyatt Regency Hong Kong, 67 Nathan Rd, Tsim Sha Tsui, **T** 2311 1234, **F** 2739 8701, www.hongkong.hyatt.com *MTR: Tsim Sha Tsui. Map 5, I4, p255* No ostentation or tacky ornaments, just sheer class and good taste with black marble and cream in the lobby and corridors. Rooms are equally as tastefully furnished, although a little characterless. With a good business centre, there is a decent selection of top restaurants, cafés and the Chin Chin bar with live entertainment. Low-season promotions offer rooms from $1000. (Way up the price scale is the Tai Pan Presidential Suite, named after the book by James Clavell, who stayed here.)

C Kimberley Hotel, 28 Kimberley Rd, Tsim Sha Tsui, **T** 2723 3888, **F** 2723 1318, www.kimberleyhotel.com.hk *MTR: Tsim Sha Tsui. Map 5, F5, p254* With a grand, winding entrance in the heart of shopping-land just off Nathan Rd, the 546 rooms and bathrooms are well-furnished but fairly small and, with no view to speak of, feel rather enclosed. However, it's good value, and discounts can bring prices down to $600. The hotel has a gym, business centre, jacuzzis and Chinese and Japanese restaurants.

C **Hotel Miramar**, 118-130 Nathan Rd, Tsim Sha Tsui, **T** 2368 1111, **F** 2369 1788, www.miramarhk.com *MTR: Tsim Sha Tsui. Map 5, F4, p254* In the heart of the noisy shopping area and therefore near the deafening and inconvenient roadworks, the Miramar is a good standard business hotel with rooms off-season available from $800. The 525 well-equipped rooms (IDD, cable TV, TV internet, kettle and minibar) are pretty similar in size, but the cheaper ones are on the lower floors and therefore have a lousy view. (Around 50% extra for a view over Kowloon Park.) The hotel has four restaurants, an indoor pool, fitness centre and separate saunas for men and women.

D **Royal Windsor**, 39 Kimberley Rd, Tsim Sha Tsui, **T** 2739 5665, **F** 2311 5101, www.windsorhotel.com.hk *MTR: Tsim Sha Tsui. Map 5, F6, p254* This 166-room hotel is not particularly flashy but presentable, neat and predictable, with a business centre and characterless restaurant. The cheapest rooms are small and have a view over Kimberley Road, with simple decor and kettle, IDD, cable TV and internet access, with larger rooms further up the price scale. Off-season low occupancy rooms are available from $580.

D **YMCA**, The Salisbury, 41 Salisbury Rd, Tsim Sha Tsui, **T** 2268 7888, **F** 2739 9315, ymcahk.org.hk *MTR: Tsim Sha Tsui. Map 5, J3, p255* Right next to the Peninsula and a whole lot cheaper. Hardly your typical YMCA but a well-finished, great value hotel with 363 rooms. The double rooms are of a decent size with attractive furnishings, IDD and voicemail, private fax line, fridge and cable TV, and two restaurants, a fitness centre, two pools and many sports facilities, plus children's playground and library.

Sleeping

F **Dadol Hotel**, 1/F Champagne Court, 16-20 Kimberley Rd, Tsim Sha Tsui, **T** 2369 8882, **F** 2311 2025. *Map 5, F5, p254* No English sign to this good value little guesthouse, but walk though the main entrance to the building, turn right and go up one floor. The 41 rooms are small, neat and clean, with assorted sizes for doubles and triples, and have cable TV, phone and a decent bathroom. It is friendly and decent English is spoken by the woman who runs it. A tiny kitchen which guests may use, with generous discounts for stays of more than 6 nights. A good safe option for women alone.

Jordan, Yau Ma Tei and Mongkok

D **Eaton Hotel**, 380 Nathan Rd, Jordan, **T** 2710 1828, **F** 2771 0043, www.eaton-hotel.com *MTR: Jordan*. A glass and steel structure towering above the highways of Kowloon, the Eaton is an efficient and well-equipped hotel popular with business travellers. Service is excellent, and the 468 rooms are a decent size with internet access, cable TV, fridge and kettle, and the Yat Tung Heen restaurant is renowned for its Cantonese cuisine. Generous discounts are available in the low season, with rooms for around $700.

D **Majestic Hotel**, 348 Nathan Rd, Jordan, **T** 2781 1333, **F** 2781 1773, www.majestichotel.com.hk *MTR: Jordan*. An imposing 15-storey building with ornate Chinese decor in the lobby lounge, the Majestic houses a huge shopping complex and like the others in the vicinity, very close to the Jade and Temple Street markets. The 387 rooms are all the same size, lower priced on the lower floors, with cable TV, kettle, minibar and safe, and the hotel contains a business centre, gym and restaurant.

D **Royal Plaza Hotel**, 193 Prince Edward Rd West, Mongkok, **T** 2982 8822, **F** 2606 0088, www.royalplaza.com.hk *MTR: Prince*

Edward. Adjacent to Mongkok KCR, this is perfect access for the train to China. The large yet soulless marble lobby lounge and enormous forecourt is popular with Chinese businessmen, and the rooms are a good size and efficient service. A good location next to the bird and flower markets, plus shopping centre with cinemas, and handy bus all the way down Nathan Rd.

E **Evergreen Hotel**, 48 Woo Sung St, Yau Ma Tei, **T** 2780 4222, **F** 2385 8584, www.evergreenhotel.com *MTR: Jordan.* A well-run little hotel, in between Nathan Rd and Temple St, with clean average-sized rooms and tasteful simple decor, but no view. Rooms include IDD phone, TV, bath, fridge and kettle, and there are fax and internet facilities in hotel. Price includes breakfast (eggs, toast and juice) and the café is open until 1700 for snacks and drinks.

E **Nathan Hotel**, 378 Nathan Rd, Jordan, **T** 2388 5141, **F** 2770 4262, nathanhk@hkstar.com *MTR: Jordan. Map 5, B4, p254* One of a handful of mid-range hotels in a small area, the Nathan is great value for money with large well-equipped rooms, although pretty sterile. There is a small business centre, and restaurants serving Chinese and European food.

E **New King's Hotel**, 473 Nathan Rd, Yau Ma Tei, **T** 2780 1281, **F** 2782 1833, newkings@netvigator.com *MTR: Yau Ma Tei.* This represents good value for money, as the rooms have better furnishings and are larger than others in this price category. Very close to Yau Ma Yei MTR, Nathan Rd and Temple St, all rooms have views over Nathan Rd, and fridge, safe and hairdryer. No restaurant in the hotel, but staff will order takeaway food and serve in the room.

E **New San Diego Hotel**, 1-5 Chi Wo St, Yau Ma Tei, **T** 2710 4888, **F** 2710 4889. *MTR: Jordan. Map 5, A5, p254* Don't be discouraged by the horse's head in the entrance, this hotel of 102 rooms is relatively smart and efficient. Standard doubles are a decent size with modern furnishings, with kettle, minibar and fridge, and the hotel has a restaurant serving western food.

F **Grand Palace Hotel**, 1B Wing Sing Lane, Yau Ma Tei, **T** 2771 8088, **F** 2771 8812. *MTR: Yau Ma Tei.* Just off Nathan Rd and a few minutes' walk from Yau Ma Tei MTR, all the 54 rooms here are minuscule and windowless, but clean and adequate for a couple of nights with a TV, phone and small shower. At least it's relatively quiet. There is a café/bar on the first floor, with a small balcony.

F **Hakkas Guest House**, Flat L 3/F Wah Fung Building, 300 Nathan Rd, Jordan, **T** 2771 3656, **F** 2770 1470. *MTR: Jordan.* *Map 5, B4, p254* The rooms come in all shapes and sizes, although none are exactly huge, but cleaner and better furnished than most others in the building. The tiled floors are clean, and although there is little English spoken it is friendly. "No hookers", promised the lady in charge. Try to see all rooms available before booking.

F-G **Tohou Hotel**, 4/F Flat G, Wah Fung Building, 300 Nathan Rd, Jordan, **T** 2770 9323, **F** 2388 2991. *MTR: Jordan.* *Map 5, B4, p254* Their business card optimistically advertises deluxe suites, but the rooms here are still tiny and vary in size so look before booking if possible, or specify the largest room available. Rooms contain phone, TV (local channels only), a tiny window (but no view) and shower. Some English is spoken, and it's slightly better organized than most of the real cheapies.

G **Hoi Shing Hotel**, Flat C, 1/F Wah Fung Building, 300 Nathan Rd, Jordan, **T** 2388 9317, **F** 2388 8659. *MTR: Jordan.* *Map 5, B4, p254* The building contains some of Hong Kong's cheapest rooms, similar in price and standard to the infamous Chungking Mansions but without the touts and the crowded lifts. The Hoi Shing is well-signposted from the main entrance and rooms are cupboard-like and basic, but just manage to fit in a toilet and shower. Suitable for a night or two, but not much more. No English spoken but friendly, and the lady will do your laundry. There are a total of 15 rooms through three separate entrances.

G Nathan House, 10/F Flat G, Wah Fung Building, 300 Nathan Rd, Jordan, **T** 2384 0143, **F** 2398 3519. *MTR: Jordan. Map 5, B4, p254* The faux wooden pillars and gold sign at the tiny reception area give a slightly unrealistic atmosphere of grandeur, but the rooms are clean if a little small, and come in assorted sizes. The place is fairly well run and maintained, with the usual basic facilities in the rooms like TV, phone, toilet and shower cubicle.

New Territories

C Royal Park Hotel, 8 Pak Hok Ting St, Sha Tin, **T** 2601 2111, www.royalpark.com.hk Near the centre of Sha Tin so convenient for travel to and from China. Essentially a large, impersonal hotel for business travellers, it has 448 rooms with the usual facilities like IDD and cable TV, and two pools, a gym, sauna and shuttle bus service to airport, Tsim Sha Tsui and Mongkok.

Lantau

Brilliant Holiday, Shop KC, Lower Deck, Mui Wo Pier, Lantau, **T** 2984 2662, **F** 2984 2110. *1100-2000.* A booking counter on the right-hand-side as you exit the ferry, offering discounted rates for the Silvermine Beach Hotel (from $400 weekdays), as well as many other cheap holiday homes. From $120.

D Silvermine Beach Hotel, 648 Silvermine Bay, Mui Wo, **T** 2984 8295, **F** 2984 1907, www.resort.com.hk The best hotel on the island, with smart doubles, some with sea view. Facilities include large terrace bar and restaurant, outdoor swimming pool, tennis courts, gym, broadband internet and IDD in the rooms, sauna and steam room. Friendly service and peaceful location overlooking the beach. Price includes buffet breakfast. Huge discounts off-season and packages per month.

F Fair View Inn, DD 328, 17D Tong Fuk, **T** 2980 2525 and 2980 2736, **F** 2980 2015. *On the main road in a small village*. A holiday home with simple, small rooms which offer good rates on weekdays. It is clean and quiet and with good access to Lantau sights and the airport. Higher price for sea view.

F Mui Wo Inn, Silvermine Bay, **T** 2984 7225, **F** 2984 1916. *Near the Seaview Holiday Resort*. Don't be discouraged by the tacky plaster statues on the veranda – this small guest-house has some gorgeous rooms with small balcony and sea view, which is worth the extra cost. The bathrooms are a decent size, and there is a small café downstairs selling snacks. Higher price and busier at weekends.

G SG Davis Hostel, Ngong Ping, **T** 2985 5610. Reservations made to IYHF Head Office, Rm 225-227, Block 19, Shek Kip Mei Estate, Kowloon, **T** 2788 1638, **F** 2788 3105, www.yha.org.hk *Bus #2 from Mui Wo, or #23 from Tung Chung. Five minutes walk from the Big Buddha*. This clean hostel is a great base for walks around the area. Renovated in 2001, it has 46 beds mostly in dorms, with a few double/family rooms which get booked up quickly. Membership to IYHF necessary, either from home country or directly from the hostel. Facilities are clean, with a kitchen and barbecue pits.

G Seaview Holiday Resort, 11 Tung Wan Tau Rd, Silvermine Bay, **T** 2984 8877, **F** 2984 8787, www.seaviewholiday.com Set back from the beach, this small friendly holiday home gets busy at weekends. The room size varies widely, and it may be better to get a huge family room for a little extra. There are 40 simple clean rooms, and a small bar and terrace restaurant serving a good value barbecue every night. Located past the Silvermine Beach hotel, it is a 10-minute walk to the airport bus.

Lamma

F **Bali Holiday Resort**, G/F 8 Main St, Yung Shue Wan, **T** 2982 4580, **F** 2982 1044. Sat back from the main street and near the restaurants and bars, the rooms here are a decent size although those with balconies offer uninspiring views to the sea and Lamma power station. Modern, decent furnishings with TV, VCD, phone and kettle, with lovely little bathrooms and a small radiator. Prices double on Sat and holidays, and get booked up quickly. Service is not great.

F **Man Lai Wah Hotel**, 2 Po Wah Garden, Yung Shue Wan, **T** 2982 0220, **F** 2982 0349. This friendly little guest house has just 8 rooms, is in a quiet location adjacent to the ferry pier and is a short walk to the restaurants and bars of the village. The small rooms are simply and adequately furnished, with TV, phone, VCD player and kettle, and some have a balcony with sea view at a slightly higher price. Rooms get booked up quickly on Sat and holidays, when prices rise by over 50%.

G **Sunrise Holiday Resort**, 15 Yung Shue Wan Main St, **T** 2982 2626, 9055 3288 and **South York Property**, 29 Yung Shue Wan Main St, **T** 2982 0427, 9054 2437. Two accommodation booking agencies with simple rooms in holiday homes, with photographs available. Phone in advance if booking for Saturday or holiday.

Cheung Chau

D **Warwick Hotel**, East Bay, Cheung Chau, **T** 2981 0081, **F** 2981 9174, www.warwickhotel.com.hk Despite its dramatic location overlooking the beach, the exterior is gloomy and the entrance and dining area lack atmosphere. Luckily renovations to the rooms in 2003 make them very comfortable and modern, with tasteful simple decor and very good bathrooms. The balconies now have clear perspex around the rail making them safe while not spoiling the view. There is a small outdoor pool, a Chinese and western restaurant, but it's probably better to eat out. Rooms off-season from $500.

F-G **Accommodation Booking Stalls**, Praya, Cheung Chau, **T** 2981 2449. Rooms from as little as $120 weekdays to larger rooms at weekends $600. Shows photographs of each place, simple rooms with bathroom. Difficult to get a room at weekends during high season and especially during the Bun Festival.

Macau

Hotel booking agencies **Shun Tak Centre**, 200 Connaught Rd Central, Sheung Wan; **Tour Products**, Shop 316 3/F, **T** 2549 9330, **F** 2549 1506; **Macao South China Travel**, Shop 318 3/F, **T** 2815 0208, **F** 2544 9378; **Beng Seng Group**, Shop 311, **T** 2540 3838, **F** 2540 1133. Three booking agents next to ticket office and departure for Macau jetfoil, for good discounts on hotels rooms in Macau. Lowest prices on weekdays, for most mid- and top-range hotels. **G/F Arrivals hall, Ferry Terminal, Macau**. Similar discounts from those just arriving with nothing booked.

D **Pousada De Coloane**, Cheoc Van Beach, Coloane Island, **T** 882 143, **F** 882 251. A sleepy, slightly chaotic family-run hotel on Coloane Island, this oozes Portuguese charm, and is around 20 mins by taxi from the ferry terminal ($60) is in a very peaceful spot. Rooms overlook the beach, the deluxe rooms with balcony are the ones to go for. Very helpful staff and child-friendly facilities with small pool and children's paddling pool, and intercom from the deluxe rooms to reception, with a Macanese restaurant on the roof. Special deals bring deluxe rooms to around $400 weekdays.

C **Mandarin Oriental Macau**, 956-1110 Av da Amizade, **T** 567 888, **F** 594 589, (tollfree from HK, **T** 800 967 338), www.mandarinoriental.com There is major construction work adjacent to the hotel due for completion end of 2003, so check the status when booking, and check when booking a room with a view that it is not a view of a building site. A classy hotel and one of the best in Macau, with plush decor and great service, and a wide selection of restaurants (Asian and Western), cafés and bars, with a huge outdoor swimming pool, jacuzzi and spa.

E **Pousada de Mong-Ha**, Colina de Mong-Ha, **T** 515 222, **F** 556 925, www.ift.edu.mo A hotel run by the adjacent tourism school, the rooms are based on traditional houses and are simple, well equipped and uncluttered. Without the frills of a top hotel, the students make a huge effort to please, although they are not always efficient. The main drawback is that there is nowhere to eat or drink in the hotel and the location means a downhill trek down a dark road to find a restaurant. Price includes buffet breakfast. $500.

B **The Westin Resort**, 1918 Estrada de Hac Sa, Coloane, **T** 871 111, **F** 871 131, www.westin.com/macau The ultimate in decadence and space, the huge resort hotel has a large, light entrance, lobby lounge and terrace restaurant near the beach in a peaceful environment, with generous-sized rooms and all the trimmings. Guests are allowed to use the private golf club (the only one in Macau) Mon-Fri, which accounts for many of their guests especially from Japan and China. Special golfing packages are available, as well as room-only rates.

F **Florida Hotel**, 2 Beco Do Pa Ralelo, **T** 923 198. A small, basic, clean guesthouse (don't be put off by the escorts loitering in the lobby), the 55 rooms have TV and phone (local only) and small bathroom. Good central location, although hard to find, just off Av de Almeida Ribeiro on the corner of Beco and Travessa de Holo Quai. No restaurant facilities, 10 mins walk to Leal Senada.

G **Vila Universal**, Cheng Peng Building, 733 Rua da Felicidade, **T** 573 247, 375 602. Next door to the Ko Wah Hotel, this simple, though impersonal, hotel has 30 small rooms (ask for one with a window), which are sparse and clean with phone and TV. Staff on each floor make it more secure.

G **Ko Wah Hotel**, 3/F 71 Rua da Felicidade, **T** 930 755, 375 599. In the heart of the action on Felicidade, a lively street full of restaurants and shops, the "reception" is on the ground floor. With an abundance of plastic flowers and kitsch decorations, the rooms are clean and basic and even have a view of the busy street. Staff are friendly but not much English is spoken. Ask to see all available rooms, as they vary in size.

F **Hotel Masters**, 162 Rua das Lorchas, **T** 937 572, **F** 937 565. A great value, well-run hotel with decent facilities like café/lobby bar and money exchange at reception. The rooms have dark wood furniture and plain interior and although the curtains may be a little tatty, they are clean and a decent size. Located near the docks, the area is a little more downmarket than Rua da Felicidade, but has character. Available from booking agents in Hong Kong. Suites available for $420. Recommended.

The beauty of eating in Hong Kong is that you can dine on nearly every cuisine in the world, from Asian to French and American to Russian, with prices ranging from a few dollars to a few hundred. But this really is the place to experience Chinese cuisine in its many varieties and sometimes the tastiest, freshest food around is in the *dai pai dongs* (cooked food markets). Some of these places have English menus, but often you have to take a few chances and try things you wouldn't dream of eating at home. Central, especially Lan Kwai Fong and SoHo, has a huge range of international restaurants and Tsim Sha Tsui is good for Asian food, especially cheap Indian restaurants in Chungking Mansions. Some of the best mid-range restaurants for local cuisine are in Causeway Bay and Wan Chai. The best fresh seafood is on Lamma, Cheung Chau and Sai Kung. If you want to have a quiet, leisurely lunch, try to avoid 1230-1400 when office-workers pile out and invade every cheap eatery around, although there are great bargains in otherwise expensive restaurants, with fixed menus at a fraction of the usual cost.

$ **Eating codes**

Price

$$$ Over $300
$$ $150-$300
$ $150 and under
Prices refer to the cost of a two-course meal without drinks.
HH = Happy Hour.

Every visitor should experience *yum cha* ('drink tea') along with their *dim sum* ('touching the heart') – small parcels of dumplings, buns and pastries, washed down with pots of tea. Each portion consists of three or four pieces, so experiment with a few varieties. Favourites include steamed shrimp dumplings (*har qau*), deep-fried spring rolls (*tsun quen*) and steamed barbecued pork buns (*cha siu bau*). Although locals have a fondness for pig's ears, chicken's feet and entrails, there is a good choice of vegetarian restaurants. Japanese cuisine is a recent big hit here with several chains of very popular, cheap sushi bars packed in the evenings.

Central and Sheung Wan

Restaurants

$$$ **M at the Fringe**, 1/F Lower Albert Rd, Central, **T** 2877 4000. *1200-1430 Mon-Fri, 1900-2230 daily. Map 2, G7, p249* One of Hong Kong's finest restaurants, and perfect for splashing out in understated style. The decor and romantic ambience enhance the superb food, which includes slow-roasted leg of lamb, roast suckling pig or deep-fried salted cod. The pavlova is divine.

$$$ **Vong**, 25/F Mandarin Oriental, 5 Connaught Rd, Central, **T** 2522 0111. *1200-1500 Mon-Fri and 1800-2400 daily. Map 2, F9,*

▶ Café culture

Although there is no traditional café culture in Hong Kong, the nearest equivalents are American- or European-inspired chains. These include the self-service **Delifrance** (average sandwiches, good pastries), **Oliver's Super Sandwiches** (hearty sandwiches, wraps and jacket potatoes), **Pacific Coffee** (free internet access and comfy sofas) and an invasion of **Starbucks**. A more interesting option is the chain of **Saint's Alp Teahouse** (see p148), with wonderful varieties of green and fruit tea with Taiwanese food. The luxury of an English-style afternoon tea is best experienced at the **Peninsula Hotel**, the **Verandah** or the **China Tee Club**, with **Post 97** making a relaxing spot for coffee and cakes.

p249 An innovative and stylish French-Vietnamese combination. Food is matched by classy black and gold decor and superb views. Favourites include quail rubbed with Thai spices, sautéed foie gras with ginger and mango and steamed sea bass in cardamom sauce.

$$$-$$ **Alibi**, 73 Wyndham St, Central, **T** 2167 1676. *1200-late. Map 2, F6, p248* Above its very hip wine bar, the brasserie is small and chic with a tiny semi-covered terrace. Continental cuisine includes lobster salad, foie gras and steak tartar.

$$$-$$ **Aqua Restaurant and Bar**, 49 Hollywood Rd, Central, **T** 2545 3999. *Map 2, E5, p248* A sophisticated award-winning restaurant, with a contemporary interior with a great view onto SoHo. International cuisine includes mushroom and lime ravioli in coconut broth, and cumin-crusted lamb loin. Set lunch is a bargain.

$$$-$$ **Zenses**, G/F Henley Building, 5 Queen's Rd, Central, **T** 2521 8999. *1200-1500 and 1830-2300. Map 2, G10, p249* The

Beginners Guide to Chinese Cuisine

Cantonese cuisine is said to be the finest in China, specializing in fast cooking at high temperatures, steaming and stir-frying ingredients like seafood, pork and chicken which leaves the vegetables, courtesy of Buddhist and Taoist vegetarian beliefs, fresh and crunchy.

Chiu Chow uses rich sauces to accompany their food, like tangerine jam for steamed lobster, sweet bean paste with fish, and garlic and vinegar sauce for dipping duck and goose into, all washed down with pungent tea.

Shanghainese cuisine favours dumplings and noodles over rice, fish is seasoned with sugar, soy sauce and yellow wine, and everyone waits with excitement for the hairy crab season (Oct-Nov).

Pekingese cuisine originates from the imperial courts, spiced with coriander, peppers and garlic and also using noodles and dumplings, with the splendid Peking Duck as it pièce de resistance.

Szechuan (Sichuan) dishes are some of China's spiciest. Smoked and simmered, blending the tastes of Thailand and India, frying chilli and melding with garlic and ginger. Favourites include smoked duck and tofu – and menus will always indicate how hot the dishes are.

Zen-like classy ambience is helped by a neon-topped long glass bar with large red lampshades hanging overhead, and dark wooden floors. Asian cuisine has a contemporary twist, like foie gras chiu chow style, crab meat with mango and avocado and curry mayonnaise, and baked seabass with pumpkin puree.

$$ **2 Sardines**, 43 Elgin St, Central, **T** 2973 6618. *1200-1430 and 1800-2230. Map 2, E4, p248* More than simply sardines, this offers a good range of classic French food. Small and relaxed.

$$ **China Lan Kwai Fong**, 17-22 Lan Kwai Fong, Central, **T** 2536 0968. *1200-1500 and 1830-2300.* *Map 2, G6, p248* A great place to experience Chinese food, its contemporary cuisine takes influences from all regions and it is set in a beautiful nostalgic interior of dark wood and birdcages complete with chirruping birds. Famous for its dim sum, and also offers great value lunch and dinner menus and a buffet brunch at weekends.

$$ **El Pomposo**, 4 Tun Wo Lane, Central, **T** 2869 7679. *Map 2, E6, p248* One of four adjacent small restaurants and bars in an alleyway, owned by the 1997 group. El Pomposo takes Spanish tapas and adds a twist, like the pork, apple and sage wontons, but also makes a grand seafood paella.

$$ **Emporio Armani Caffe HK**, 2/F Chater House, 11 Chater Rd, Central, **T** 2532 7722. *1130-2230.* *HH 1700-2000.* *Map 2, F9, p249* Swathes of red plastic spiralling round the entrance hall set a designer kitsch tone: neon walls, crisp white tablecloths and high ceilings. The Italian chef conjures up delights such as deep-fried rock oysters with young spinach. Good value high tea.

$$ **Habibi's**, G/F 112-114 Wellington St, Central, **T** 2544 6198. *1200-1500, 1800-2330, closed Sun.* *Map 2, E5, p248* Dine on chicken or lamb tajine, mixed grill and hot and cold mezzes in the ornate decor of 1930s Cairo. A good choice of Arabic desserts and North African wines. All meat is halal.

$$ **Ivan the Kozak**, LG/F 46-48 Cochrane St, Central, **T** 2851 1193. *Map 2, F5, p248* Traditional Russian/Ukrainian dishes like blini and bortsch come with baked flaming piglet in vodka sauce or baked rabbit stuffed with raisins and apricots. Garish murals give a taverna-type ambience to the place, quite fitting given its 25 varieties of vodka. Service is homely and friendly, with a raucous atmosphere on Friday nights.

$$ **Pasta E Pizza**, B/F 11 Lyndhurst Terr, Central, **T** 2545 1675. *1200-1500 Mon-Fri and 1800-2300 Mon-Sat.* *Map 2, E6, p248* A cheerful, homely Italian restaurant complete with red-checked tablecloths and hearty food. Serves pizzas hot from its stone-based oven, just the way they should be, plus pastas and salads. Good value set lunches and live jazz on Saturday nights. Booking essential.

$$ **Post 97**, UG/F 9 Lan Kwai Fong, Central, **T** 2186 1837. *0930-0100 Sun-Thu, 0930-0400 Fri and Sat.* *Map 2, G7, p249* The first establishment of the 1997 Group, Post is a bar/café/restaurant that has been the backbone of Lan Kwai Fong for over a decade and is busy most nights with a cool clientele. Perfect for an afternoon coffee and cake, plate of nachos with your champagne cocktails, or the famous eggs benedict as a good hangover cure.

$$ **Yung Kee Restaurant**, 32-40 Wellington St, Central, **T** 2522 1624. *1100-2330.* *Map 2, F6, p248* This institution has been famed for its roasted goose for 50 years, and also won a recent award for preserved pig's trotters with Chinese marinade. Has a good selection of classic Cantonese dishes, and good service.

$$-$ **Luk Yu Tea House**, 24-26 Stanley St, Central, **T** 2523 5464. *0700-2200.* *Map 2, E6, p248* Ignore the surly service, enjoy one of the establishments for an authentic dim sum experience (*0700-1700*). Ornately carved wood and high ceilings ooze a timeless atmosphere over its three floors. Main dishes include pigeon, fried frog's legs and spiced pig's tongue.

$ **Eating Plus**, 1/F 1009 International Finance Center, Central, **T** 2868 0599. *Map 2, D8, p249* A funky venue popular with office workers in the IFC, the emphasis here is on healthy, tasty and good value Asian food. Vietnamese beef noodles, vegetarian laksa and baked cheesecake with mango mousse is an ideal way to fill up before boarding the airport express, in the same building.

$ **Fotogalerie**, Fringe Club, 2/F 2 Lower Albert Rd, Central, **T** 2521 7251. *1200-2300, closed Sun.* *Map 2, G7, p249* Wonderful location and value for a wholesome tasty buffet lunch, *1200-1400, Mon-Fri*, plus tapas and light meals, *1400-2230*. On Friday and Saturday evenings the tiny rooftop terrace has a barbecue buffet, overlooked by Central's tower blocks. A bohemian atmosphere, interesting art and photo exhibitions and live music downstairs.

$ **Good Luck Thai Food**, G/F 13 Wing Wah Lane, Central, **T** 2877 2971. *0800-0200.* *Map 2, F6, p248* Dining out in a grubby courtyard in an alleyway near ultra hip Lan Kwai Fong, tucking into tom yam soup or chicken with ginger and basil still seems to be popular, especially when people start spilling out of the bars.

$ **Koshary**, G/F Shop A, 112-114 Wellington St, Central, **T** 2544 3886. *1030-2400.* *Map 2, E5, p248* The café version of next-door Habibi's serves traditional Middle Eastern street food like fatoush and grilled halloumi. Taste a good range of Egyptian flavours with a plate of mixed hot and cold starters. All meat is halal.

$ **Sheung Wan Gala Plaza**. *1800-2400.* *Map 2, A2, p248* Sheung Wan's waterfront was redeveloped in early 2003 into a nightly collection of stalls, entertainment and food. The crowded outdoor tables are surrounded by food stalls selling crabs, huge prawns, mussels and more, along with simple dishes of noodles and vegetables, with beer and soft drinks. Great fun, especially for kids.

Cafés

$ **China Tee Club**, 1/F Pedder Building, 12 Pedder St, Central, **T** 2521 0233. *Map 2, F8, p249* Although the portions are rather small, afternoon tea ($80) here is a blissful way to rest weary feet in the heart of Central, with a huge selection of English and Chinese teas in something resembling a colonial drawing room.

$ **The Mix**, Standard Chartered Bank Building, Central, **T** 2523 7396. (Also at International Finance Center, Central, **T** 2971 0688, and Hoi Kwong St, Quarry Bay, **T** 2562 7313). *0700-1930. Map 2, G10, p249* Fresh smoothies, juices, sandwiches and wraps come in huge sizes in this large bright self-service café. Large sofas, magazines, and even listening stations for the CDs on sale.

$ **Pier 3 Garden View Restaurant**, roof garden of Discovery Bay Ferry Pier (no 3), Central. *1000-2000. Map 2, A8, p249* An undiscovered gem on the top of the pier. Popular with old ladies in the mornings prasticing tai chi, it's hard to believe this is in Central. Simple noodles dishes, Chinese snacks, beer, and friendly service.

$ **T W Café**, Shop 2, G/F Capitol Plaza, 2-10 Lyndhurst Terr, Central, **T** 2544 2237 and 1/F 2 Queen Victoria St, Central, **T** 2522 9795. *Map 2, E6, p248* This is a rarity: a blissful range of coffees from around the world, served with sandwiches and cakes in something resembling a tiny European café.

$ **XTConICE Gelato**, 45 Cochrane St, Central. *1200-2400 Sun-Tue, Thu; 1200-0400 Fri and Sat. Map 2, E5, p248* This tiny Italian-style ice-cream store, near many bars and restaurants, boasts unusual combinations like ginger and cinnamon, toasted almond and green apple sorbet. Free samples in case you can't decide.

Admiralty, Wan Chai

Restaurants

$$$ **Kokage**, Starcrest, 9 Star St, Wan Chai, **T** 2529 6138. *1200-1500 Mon-Fri and 1800-2400 daily. Map 3, G4, p250* Innovative Japanese cuisine in a hip part of town, immersed in dark wood and candlelight. Savour the miso-glazed butterfish with taro, crabmeat

tempura, or 6-hour roasted suckling pig with miso clam broth, all in a sumptuous atmosphere with attentive service.

$$ **Amaroni's Little Italy**, 213 Queen's Rd East, Wan Chai, T 2891 8855. *1100-2400.* *Map 3, H8, p251* *See p148.*

$$ **R66**, 62/F Hopewell Centre, 183 Queen's Rd East, Wan Chai, T 2862 6166. *1200-2300. HH 1700-2000.* *Map 3, H7, p251* The city's only revolving restaurant (takes 66 minutes for each revolution) but come for the view, not the food. The best option is to enjoy afternoon tea (1430-1800) while gazing at the panorama of the city and surrounding hills. The unappetizing buffet lunch and dinner include sushi, noodles and western dishes.

$$ **Ye Shanghai**, Level 3 Pacific Pl, 88 Queensway, Admiralty. T 2918 9833. *1130-1500, 1800-2400.* *Map 3, F2, p250* *See p147*

$$-$ **American Peking Restaurant**, 20 Lockhart Rd, Wan Chai, T 2527 1000. *Map 3, F6, p250* An establishment that has been popular for years, ever since the American servicemen used the area for R&R in the 1950s. The cuisine is essentially Pekingese, so a great place to sample the famous Peking Duck. A huge restaurant with portions to match.

$ **Healthy Mess Vegetarian Garden**, 51-53 Hennessy Rd, Wan Chai, T 2527 3918. *1030-2300.* *Map 3, F6, p250* With emphasis on the healthy, this popular informal restaurant serves a big selection of vegetarian Chinese dishes including dim sum (eat in or takeaway). It has a wide variety of fake meat, fried noodles with asparagus, water chestnuts and baby corn, thick tofu soup. Service is fast and friendly.

$ **The Open Kitchen**, 6/F Hong Kong Arts Centre, 2 Harbour Rd, Wan Chai, T 2827 2923. *1100-2200, 1100-2300 Fri.* *Map 3, D6, p250* A self-service restaurant on the 6th floor commands a stunning view of the harbour, and the contemporary decor makes the most of it, with bar stools in front of the huge windows. Food is tasty and varied, with good-value pastas, steaks and grilled ostrich steak, and the Indian chef is best known for his laksa, a spicy thick soup.

Causeway Bay, Happy Valley and North Point

Restaurants

$$ **Brown**, 18A Sing Woo Rd, Happy Valley, **T** 2891 8558. *1130-0200 Mon-Fri, 1000-0200 Sat-Sun. Map 1, D4, p247* A rarity in these parts, with comfortable seating on the terrace and the perfect place to enjoy the huge brunch served at weekends. A relaxed and friendly atmosphere and a good menu for dinner.

$$ **Hong Kong Old Restaurant**, B/F Newton Hotel, 218 Electric Rd, North Point, **T** 2508 1081. *Map 1, C5, p247 See p147*

$ **Beppu Menkan**, 3 Pak Sha Rd, Causeway Bay, **T** 2881 0831. *Map 4, E5, p247 See p147*

$ **Kung Tak Lam**, G/F Lok Sing Centre, 51 Yee Wo St, Causeway Bay, **T** 2890 3127, 1/F 45-47 Carnarvon Rd, Tsim Sha Tsui, **T** 2367 7881. *Map 4, D8, p253* One of the best vegetarian restaurants in town, specializing in Shanghainese cuisine which is heavy on breads, hotpots and dumplings. Their food contains no MSG and professes to be suitable for diabetics, using pesticide-free products, including organic honey and vegetables available for takeaway.

$ **Saint's Alp Teahouse**, 470 Lockhart Rd, Causeway Bay, **T** 2147 0389. *Map 4, D3, p252 See p148*

Cafés

$ **Deli Bess**, 160 Electric Rd, North Point, **T** 2512 8007. *0800-2000.*
Map 1, C5, p247 A tiny friendly café making fresh sandwiches,
salads, baked potatoes and toasties, washed down with a great
selection of teas, coffees and juices. Simple and tasty.

Shau Kei Wan, Sai Wan Ho and Chai Wan

$ **Dai Pai Dong**, 57 Shau Kei Wan St East. *0800-2000.* *Map 1, C7,
p247* Dirt cheap, lively dai pai dong, with basic noodle dishes (no
English menu) ideal to fill up en route to the museums. Basic
English spoken, can cook to request if vegetarian. No English
name, but near the "Bonky Parking" sign.

The Peak

Restaurants

$$ **Café Deco**, Peak Galleria, 118 Peak Rd, **T** 2849 5111. *1130-2400
Sun-Thu, 1130-0100 Fri and Sat.* *Map 1, D2, p247* Best loved for its
huge windows overlooking the harbour, the art deco-inspired
interior looks clean and slick. Enjoy the city lights with sushi, oysters
and Asian salads, or a lunchtime burger or baguette.

$$ **The Peak Lookout**, 121 Peak Rd, **T** 2849 1000. *1030-2330
Sun-Thu, 1030-0100 Fri and Sat; weekends and public holidays opens
0830.* *Map 1, D2, p247* Formerly the famous Peak Café, this Hong
Kong establishment. Serves up sumptuous food, on a delightful
terrace at one of the highest points of the city. The Hainan chicken
rice and New Zealand baby lamb rack represent the international

cuisine, with warm-centred chocolate cake a perfect end to dinner. Great for afternoon tea or even breakfast.

$ **Café De Mon Ton**, 21 Level 2, Peak Galleria, 118 Peak Rd, **T** 2848 5650. *Map 1, D2, p247* A bizarre combination of Italian and western Japanese, offering Japanese curries alongside pasta dishes, in a tiny and charming café with simple furnishings.

$ **Marché**, Peak Tower level 6 & 7, 128 Peak Rd, **T** 2849 2000. *1100-2300, weekends 0900-2300. Map 1, D2, p247* The tacky decor – a huge red cow awaits you at the entrance – is amply compensated for by the views. Styled like a marketplace, there are choices of salad buffet, Asian noodle dishes, fresh pasta, sushi and of course ice cream (the restaurant is owned by Movenpick). Enjoy half-price drinks, *1600-1900*, on sleek bar stools at the huge windows. There's a wonderful children's play/eating area too.

South Hong Kong Island

Restaurants

$$$ **The Verandah**, The Repulse Bay Hotel, 109 Repulse Bay Rd, Repulse Bay, **T** 2812 2722. *Map 1, F5, p247* A truly romantic dining experience, in a luxurious colonial setting with 20 tables clad in crisp white cotton, high ceiling fans and a fabulous sea view. The French menu includes fillet of venison scented with green tea, black pepper steak cooked at your table, and Boston lobster salad. Also serves afternoon tea, *1500-1730*, and the buffet Sunday lunch, *1100-1430*, is hugely popular – booking essential. Smart casual dress required.

$$ **Black Sheep**, 452 Shek O Village, **T** 2809 2021. *1300-2230. Map 1, F7, p247* This tiny but stylish restaurant with tasteful decor looks

more like a simple café, although the menu is anything but. Wonderful soups are followed by grilled lamb chops with thyme or sea bass fillet. Booking necessary at weekends.

$$ **Spices**, G/F The Repulse Bay Hotel, 109 Repulse Bay Rd, Repulse Bay, **T** 2812 2711. *1200-1430, 1830-2230.* *Map 1, F5, p247* Adjacent to The Verandah, but with the advantage of a terrace (and cheaper), the menu offers Thai, Vietnamese and Indian dishes with plenty of vegetarian options. A tasteful interior and smart service.

$ **Bamboo**, Temple Sq (off Shek O Village Rd), **T** 2809 2021. *1100-2300. Planet Time open till 0200 Fri and Sat.* *Map 1, F7, p247* Opposite a beautiful little Tin Hau temple with frescos on the outer walls, Bamboo is the sister restaurant of Black Sheep and opened in 2002. Their speciality is pizzas, cooked in a wood burning stove. At the back is Planet Time, a very small, tacky bar/disco.

$ **Shek O Chinese and Thailand Seafood Restaurant**, 303 Shek O Village, **T** 2809 4426. *1130-2200.* *Map 1, F7, p247* Popular with the wealthy expat population and day trippers and packed at weekends, this cheerful eatery serves up shrimps with garlic, Thai soups and curries and Shanghai noodles.

Tsim Sha Tsui

Restaurants

$$$ **Felix**, 28/F The Peninsula Hotel, Salisbury Rd, **T** 2315 3188. *1800-0200.* *Map 5, K4, p255* Settle down for romantic cocktails 28 floors high in the stylish Phillipe Starck-designed interior, and gaze at the view although the harbour view from the men's toilets is, apparently, even better. Not that this should detract from the food, as Felix serves Pacific Rim cuisine including Boston lobster, seared

ahi tuna and Hibachi fillet of beef on sesame spinach. The bar is popular for those unable to afford the pricey food.

$$ **Hong Kong Old Restaurant**, 4/F 1 Kimberley Rd, **T** 2722 1812. *1100-1500 and 1730-2300.*   *Map 5, F4, p254   See also p143* Noted for its excellent Shanghainese food, this large bright dining hall serves thin sliced pig's ear in spicy soy sauce, oven-smoked pigeon, spicy prawns with chilli and garlic, and steamed sea crab in yellow wine sauce.

$$ **Ye Shanghai**, 6/F Marco Polo Hongkong Hotel, Harbour City, **T** 2376 3322. *1130-1500 and 1800-2400.*   *Map 5, J2, p255   See also p141* In a stylish mix of art deco and Chinese designs inspired by 1930s Shanghai, feast on Jiangsu and Zhejang cuisine as well as Shanghainese. Strong on seafood, dishes include sautéed baby river shrimp, deep fried yellow fish and Shanghai hairy crab. The Admiralty branch has large windows and takeaway service.

$$-$ **Gaylord**, 1/F Ashley Centre, 23-25 Ashley Rd, **T** 2376 1001. *1200-1500 Mon-Sat, 1300-1500 Sun, 1800-2300 daily.*   *Map 5, I3, p255* Hong Kong's oldest Indian restaurant hasn't lost its touch. Newly refurbished and classy yet comfortable, the food is all freshly made and there's a great variety of meat and vegetarian dishes. Live music in the evenings, and a good value set lunch Mon-Sat.

$ **Beppu Menkan**, G/F 107 Chatham Rd South, **T** 2736 8700. *1130-2400.*   *Map 5, E7, p254* Near the Art Museum this is a good place to drop in for lunch. An informal Japanese noodle bar, it does great ramen (thick spicy noodle soup), and also has a small selection of sashimi and rice set meals. Great value and pleasant service, with branches at Causeway Bay and Mongkok.

$ **Taj Mahal Club**, 3/F B4, B Block Chunking Mansions, Nathan Rd, **T** 2722 5454. *1130-2400.*   *Map 5, I/J5, p255* One of the best Indian choices inside the 17 floors of grimy mayhem. Fresh biriyanis, paneer with garlic, and mutton Taj special. Wash it all down with mango lassi, or a masala chai. Take the staircase on the extreme left of the ground floor, rather than braving the cramped lift.

Cafés

$$ **The Peninsula**, Salisbury Rd, **T** 2920 2888. *Map 5, K4, p255* It seems sinful to place such a decadent establishment in the "café" section but high tea, complete with sandwiches and cakes, taken in the lobby, to the sweeping sounds from the string quartet, is a must.

Jordan, Yau Ma Tei and Mongkok

$ **Beppu Menkan**, 242 Sai Yeung Choi St South, Mongkok, **T** 3281 6611. *See p147*

$ **Saint's Alp Teahouse**, 23 Soy St, Mongkok, **T** 2710 7712, and 1K Nanking St, Jordan, **T** 2783 8582. With dozens of branches across the territory, this chain of cheery informal Taiwanese teahouses offers a great selection, like ruby grapefruit black tea with citron agar, helping to revive the appreciation of this noble beverage. They also serve cheap noodle and meat dishes.

Wong Tai Sin, Diamond Hill and Kowloon Tong

Restaurants

$$ **Amaroni's Little Italy**, LG 132 Festival Walk, Kowloon Tong, **T** 2265 8818. *1100-2400. MTR/KCR: Kowloon Tong.* Classic American Italian cuisine, which means huge portions and food for sharing.

The fantastic thin-crust pizzas are ample for two, and there is a good selection of pastas and salads. A wonderfully lively atmosphere, with rows of white-clothed tables, walls plastered with Italian film posters and friendly service.

$ **Lucky House Seafood Restaurant**, 1/F, Wong Tai Sin Shopping Centre, Wong Tai Sin, **T** 2327 7118. *0630-2200. MTR: Wong Tai Sin. Follow signs in the shopping centre to "Chinese Restaurant".* Great dim sum, *0630-1630*. Chaotic and atmospheric. Little English spoken so it may be a question of pointing and taking a chance.

$ **Perfect Vegetarian Cuisine**, LG6 Lung Chung Mall, 136 Lung Cheung Rd, Wong Tai Sin, **T** 2412 0888. *0700-2300. MTR: Wong Tai Sin.* A large bright restaurant with Buddhist-style Chinese vegetarian food, specializing in rich, fake meat dishes. In addition, it has a selection of dim sum (also available for takeaway).

New Territories

Restaurants

$$ **Jaspa's**, 13 Sha Tsui Path, Sai Kung, **T** 2792 6388. *1000-late, 0900-late Sun.* One of Sai Kung's most popular restaurants, with a stylish modern interior of orange picture-filled walls, and a few tables outside opposite the old ladies playing cards. International menu and a highly recommended pavlova.

$ **Chung Chuk Lam Shanghai Restaurant**, 24 Man Nin St, Sai Kung, **T** 2792 6883. *1100-2200*. With many seafood restaurants in the area, this is a good alternative with cheap and hearty Shanghainese food, like dumpling, noodle and vegetarian dishes. A rather inconspicuous entrance, but don't be discouraged.

Cafés

$ **Ali Oli's**, 11 Sha Tsui Path, Sai Kung, **T** 2792 2655. *0700-1900*.
Famous bakery and café next door to Jaspa's. Sells cakes, bread,
sandwiches and pastries, like pumpkin, pinenut and rosemary
bread and blueberry custard Danish. Good to stock up for a picnic
or walk. Also sells hiking guides and maps.

$ **Coffee Mill**, Shop 56 Sai Kung Villa, 22-40 Fuk Man Rd, Sai
Kung, **T** 2792 2132. *0800-1930*. A small friendly café near the bus
terminal, with a good range of fresh coffee and snacks, cheesecake
and sandwiches, plus a simple breakfast menu.

$ **Wong's Kitchen and Café**, 28 Pai Tau Village, Sha Tin, **T** 2601
3218. *0730-2100*. *KCR: Sha Tin*. This cosy café feels like Mr Wong's
tiny living room, tucked away at the end of an old row of village
houses (village signposted from Sha Tin KCR station). Simple and
homely food: breakfast, sandwiches and noodles.

Lantau

$$ **Golden Siam Thai Cuisine**, B13 Tung Chung City Gate, Tung
Chung, **T** 2109 4418. *1130-1600 and 1800-2300*. A huge bright
restaurant in the basement of a shopping centre. Curry crab, fried
crab with ginger and green onion and deep fried pomfret with sweet
chilli sauce, with plenty of meat and vegetarian dishes.

$$-$ **The Gallery**, 26 Tong Fuk, Lantau, **T** 2980 2582. *1100-2230,
closed Mon (open public holidays)*. With a Middle Eastern theme, the
Gallery has a good selection of dips and starters and the
ever-popular outdoor grill gets smoking for fish, steak and lamb
rack. A good choice of wines in the bar, it gets busy at weekends
and holidays so reservations recommended.

$$-$ The Stoep, 32 Lower Cheung Sha Village, **T** 2980 2699. *1100-2200 (last orders) closed Mon (open public holidays).* Mediterranean and South African cuisine on the waterfront. Popular at weekends and holidays (reservations advised). Snack on dips with their famous home-made bread and soup, or go for "Dolla's Braai", a huge portion (enough for two) of barbecued meats.

$ Chung Lok Yuen, 14A Nam Chung, Tai O. *1100-2000. Turn left at the large bamboo structure on entering Tai O, take the left fork at the kids' playground and past the Hoi Wan.* Difficult to find, but worth it for good, no frills Cantonese food. On left is a sign in Chinese, red letters on yellow. Food is fresh and the boss speaks a little English. Specializes in fake meat and good fried rice.

$ Fook Moon Lam, Tai O Market St. This restaurant gets the crowds in at weekends and is one of the most popular for fresh seafood. Large and cheerful with English menu.

$ Hei Gei, 56 Mui Wo Rural Committee Rd, Cheung Chau, Mui Wo. *0730-2100.* This is one of several great cheap restaurants on the street, popular with locals for breakfast or a bowl of noodles after work. English-language menu, offering noodles, rice, spicy Singapore and Vietnamese dishes.

$ Melody Inn Thai Cuisine, 10 Ha Leng Pei Chueng, Tung Chung, **T** 2988 8129. *1100-1400, 1800-2230.* A pleasant alternative to Tung Chung shopping centre, this family-run restaurant is a gem with fresh tasty seafood, soups and vegetarian noodle dishes, all served up with a smile and cheap wine. Because of the location (out of the way in the old part of the town), telephone and they will collect from the airport or Tung Chung MTR.

$ Tea Garden Restaurant, opposite SG Davis Hostel, Ngong Ping, **T** 2985 5161. If you don't fancy the dining hall din of Po Lin

Monastery (see p96), this scruffy garden café is relaxed and serves up standard Cantonese dishes. Nothing elaborate – mainly rice, noodles, soup and fried chicken. Cheap and cheerful.

$ **Yee Hen**, 1 Mui Wo Cooked Food Market, **T** 2984 2778. By far the best food in the area. Its great Cantonese food ranges from fresh seafood to the wonderful claypots, which come to your table bubbling and steaming. Friendly, informal and cheap, it is popular with locals, but tourists rarely venture here.

Lamma

$ **Bookworm Café**, 79 Yung Shue Wan Main St, **T** 2982 4838. *1000-1900, 0900-2100 weekends and holidays.* New Age haven with wholesome food, brunch, soups and cakes. A good selection of second-hand books, internet access (50c/min) and a popular place to sip coffee and read the paper. Very child-friendly.

$ **Concerto Inn Garden Café**, 28 Hung Shing Ye Beach, **T** 2982 1668. With a fabulous location on the small beach, the terrace café is part of the hotel and has a varied menu of soups, vegetarian, Indonesian, Singaporian and Japanese main dishes.

$ **Deli Lamma**, 36 Yung Shue Wan Main Street, **T** 2982 1583. One of the better venues along this street packed with endless tourist-friendly restaurants, Deli has strong Indian flavours like tandoori chicken, as well as pizzas, pastas and good breakfasts.

$ **Han Lok Yuen**, 16-17 Hung Shing Ye, **T** 2982 0680. *1130-2030, Sun 1130-1900, closed Mon.* This famous pigeon restaurant has an idyllic setting overlooking Hung Shing beach, although not improved by ferocious mosquitoes, popular with weekend junk boat day trippers. Roast pigeon is served whole, and the minced quail also comes recommended.

$ **Sampan Seafood Restaurant**, 16 Yung Shue Wan Main Street, **T** 2982 2388. *1000-2330*. A large noisy and cheerful Chinese restaurant with tables near the waterfront, it serves up dim sum, clams, prawns and garoupa, the usual rice and noodle dishes, and roast pigeon. Packed on Sundays.

Cheung Chau

$ **Hing Lok Restaurant**, 2A Pak Sha Sixth Lane. *1100-2230*. One of several seafood restaurants on the waterfront of the island, all of which are popular and pretty similar, although everyone seems to have their favourite. The deep-fried squid and crab is good, and the wine is cheap.

$ **Hometown Teahouse**, 12 Tung Wan Rd, **T** 2981 5038. *1200-2400*. A quaint, cottage-like appearance, the teahouse has just a couple of tables on the narrow street and is run by an extremely gregarious Japanese lady, eager for passers-by to taste her fresh tea, sushi and bean-filled pancakes.

Macau

$$ **Flamingo**, Hyatt Regency, 2 Estrada Almirante Marques Esparteiro, Taipa Island, **T** 831 234 ext. 1874. *1200-1500 and 1900-2300*. One of Macau's hidden gems – fantastic food in a peaceful, romantic location. Baked duck rice and coriander garlic sautéed clams, with a bottle of fine Portuguese red, tastes even sweeter when dining next to a pond of orange koi carp and ducks hoping for some of your freshly baked bread. Tranquillity with excellent service at a very reasonable price.

$$ **O Porto Interior**, 259B Rua Da Almirante Sergio, **T** 967 770. *1200-2330*. A bright friendly restaurant with interesting

photographs on the walls and unpretentious decor. Serving Portuguese and Macanese dishes, it does great fried shrimps and curries, as well as a good selection of fresh fish.

$$ **Restaurante Litoral**, 261A Rua do Almirante Sergio, **T** 967 878. *1200-1500 and 1800-2300.* Famed for its African chicken, the Litoral was one of the first restaurants run by women specializing in traditional Macanese cuisine which, as its founder says, was one of the original fusion foods of the world. Other signature dishes include stewed duck with herbs, and curried shrimp with crabmeat.

$$-$ **A Lorcha**, 289A Rua Do Almirante Serigo, **T** 313 193. *1230-1500 and 1830-2300, closed Tue.* One of Macau's most popular restaurants. It presents typical Macanese food in informal, bright surroundings with dark wooden beams. Packed at weekends (reservations recommended), locals and visitors come for king prawns grilled Macanese style, African chicken, and serradura – a waist-enhancing cream and biscuit pudding.

$ **Nga Tim Café**, 8 Rua Caetano, Coloane Village, **T** 882 086. *1200-2300.* Nga Tim (which means "a good place to relax") has hearty seafood and meat dishes with no frills, and an informal atmosphere popular with locals at weekends. Portuguese seafood rice pot, drunken prawns and salt-and-pepper crab are all washed down with a large selection of wines and draught beers.

$ **Pizzeria Toscana**, Apoio do Grande Premio de Macau, 1st Andar, Ave da Amizade, **T** 726 637. *0830-2330, closed 1st Tue every month, except public holidays.* Opposite the ferry pier, next to the Grand Prix stand, this lively informal Italian restaurant has a good stab at pizzas, pastas, risottos and meat dishes, with prima pasta and secondi piatti. Very good value, cheap local wine, and lovely displays of cheeses and antipasti.

For years it was **Lan Kwai Fong**, now the place is **SoHo**, (SOuth of HOllywood Road in Central), a new name and image for an old area. This is home to some of the sleekest bars adorned with dark wood and high ceilings, the trendiest clubs with chrome and glass, and the best-dressed night birds with Prada and Mui Mui. **Wan Chai** has always had a sleazier ambience, infamous for its plethora of hostess clubs and love hotels along Lockhart Road, but has cleaned up a little in recent years. Although still earthy, with a few hostess clubs, there is a trend for new bars whose snacks consist of tempura and satay, rather than cheese and onion crisps. **Tsim Sha Tsui**, with a high concentration of cheap hotels, has many watering holes more reminiscent of England or Australia. Drinking is expensive throughout the city (at least $35 for a standard drink), but bars do stay open late (around 0300 at weekends) and it is possible to drink and dance all night. Many bars have a dance floor with DJ at weekends, usually playing an unremarkable mix of soul, funk and R&B, and top hotel clubs often have an in-house Filipino band playing covers of soulful ballads.

★ Central bars and clubs for a night on the town

While the bad news is that drinks are pricey, the good news is that most bars offer **Happy Hours**, usually 2-for-1, which often lasts most of the afternoon until early evening. In addition to those, many bars and clubs have **Ladies Nights**, one night of the week (Mon-Thu) with free standard drinks for women in order to entice more men. Check with *HK Magazine* or *BC Magazine* for details of both. The bars around Lan Kwai Fong and D'Aguilar Street are too numerous to list or recommend here, except for some tucked away which deserve a mention, but the area is tiny enough to wander around and see what catches your eye. **NB** HH = Happy Hour

Central and Sheung Wan

Bars

Alibi, 73 Wyndham St, Central, **T** 2167 8989. *1200-late. HH 1800-2100. Map 2, F6, p248* Famous for its margheritas and martinis, this is where the chic crowd lets its hair down and may even dance round their Prada handbags. During the week it's a comfortable wine bar, on Fri and Sat the DJ plays funk and soul. Tue and Wed are Manicure nights: a manicure and two Martinis for $200.

Blue Door, 5/F 37 Cochrane St, Central, **T** 2858 6555. *Fri-Sat. Map 2, E5, p248* A new bar with live jazz on Fri and Sat only. Relaxed informal setting, its blue walls are covered with calligraphy, courtesy of the King of Kowloon (see p71). Tasty Sichuan food is available at **Yellow Door**, downstairs.

Club 64, 12-14 Wing Wah Lane, Central, **T** 2523 2801. *1430-0200 Mon-Thu, 1430-0300 Fri-Sat, 1800-0100 Sun. HH 1430-2100. Map 2, F6, p248* Attracts an arty, student, trendy crowd yet still one of the least pretentious bars in the area. Named after the June 4th Tiananmen Square killings (6/4), it has photographs, posters and flyers promoting independent artists and writers. Crowds spill out into the grubby courtyard at weekends.

Dublin Jack, 37-43 Cochrane St, Central, **T** 2543 0081. *1130-0200. HH 1200-2000. Map 2, E5, p248* Tucked under the mid-levels escalator, this cosy and comfortable Irish pub spread across three floors serves up a hearty Irish breakfast and other traditional dishes, washed down with a wide variety of ales and stouts.

Feather Boa, 38 Staunton St, Central, **T** 2857 2586. *1930-late. Map 2, E4, p248* This tiny former antique store still has a slight bordello feel with an air of faded decadence, through an inconspicuous entrance down an alleyway, but it attracts a hip crowd and has a friendly atmosphere. The whisky cocktails are good.

Fringe Club, 2 Lower Albert Rd, Central, **T** 2521 77251. *1200-2400 Mon-Thu, 1200-0300 Fri-Sat. HH 1500-2100 Mon-Thu. Map 2, G7, p249* Wonderful little club for alternative arts, music, entertainment, food and drink. Fotogalerie has a tiny terrace and rooftop, packed on Fri nights, also serving food (see p135). Ernest and Julio Gallo Gallery, on the ground floor, has live music on Fri and Sat.

Gecko, Ezra Lane, Lower Hollywood Rd, Central, **T** 2537 4680. *1800-late (closes 0300 Fri and Sat). HH 1600-2200 Tue-Thu and Sun, 1600-2100 Fri-Sat. Map 2, F5, p248* For lovers of good wine (plus absinthe and $17,000 bottles of vintage Armanac) and lounging on comfy sofas, this small bar with its candlelight and tasteful furnishings is hard to find, so has rather an exclusive feel to it. Wine-tasting twice a month and live jazz every Wed.

Le Jardin, 10 Wing Wah Lane, Central, **T** 2526 2717. *1200-0100 Mon-Wed, 1200-late Thu-Sat. HH 1200-2000. Map 2, F6, p248* In the heart of Central yet hidden away upstairs, Le Jardin has a garden setting which is something of a relief from the other chaotic bars in the area. Renowned for a jukebox which enhances, rather than detracts from, the classy atmosphere.

Music Room Live, 2/F California Entertainment Building, 34-36 D'Aguilar St, Central, **T** 2845 8477. *HH 1800-2100. Map 2, F7, p249* Previously the Jazz Club and Bar, the newly formed venue has big names in international blues and jazz, as well as salsa, Cuban and R&B. In addition to the Live Room, there's the comfortable, velvety Velvet Lounge.

Clubs

Club 97, 9 Lan Kwai Fong, Central, **T** 2810 9333. *1800-0200 Mon-Thu, 1800-0400 Fri-Sun. HH 1800-2200 Mon-Thu. Map 2, G7, p249* A longstanding institution (in a Hong Kong context that can mean anything more than five years), Club is a chilled lounge area with sophisticated sounds, gay happy hour (1800-2200 Fri) and reggae nights every Sun.

Drop, LG/F 39-43 Hollywood Rd, Central, **T** 2543 8856. *1900-0200 Mon-Tue, 1900-0300 Wed, 1900-0400 Thu, 1900-0600 Fri-Sat (members only after 2300). HH 1900-2200 Mon-Fri. Map 2, F5, p248* Best known for its fresh-fruit martinis, Drop is a chilled cocktail lounge in the early evenings and a pumping party place later on for the beautiful people, with Hong Kong's top DJs taking care of the ultra-cool music.

Edge, Shop 2 G/F The Centrium, 60 Wyndham St, Central, **T** 2523 6690. *1800-0430 Sun-Thu, 1800-0500 Fri-Sat. HH 1800-2100. Map 2, G6, p248* This huge club in a new glossy highrise has three bars, a live music room with bands every night, and a kitchen which serves food until 0200. Very popular and usually queues at weekends.

Home, 2/F 23 Hollywood Rd, Central, **T** 2545 0023. *2100-late Mon-Thu, 2100-0900 Fri-Sat. Map 2, F5, p248 See also p211* One of the cheapest places and has latest closing times in town, the assorted DJs keep the party going on Fri and Sat nights till 0900, although there are comfy sofas if you fall asleep earlier. Music ranges on different nights between R'n'B, Latin house, funk and progressive house.

Bars and clubs

Liquid, 1-5 Elgin St, Central, **T** 2549 8386. *1800-late Tue-Fri, 2000-late Sat-Sun. Map 2, E4, p248* A large good-vibe venue, it has a ground floor lounge and a basement club with dance floor. Music is usually funky house, and there are assorted offers and happy hours throughout the week, including gay happy hour, *1800-2200 Fri*, and free drinks on ladies night, *Thu*.

Propaganda, LG/F 1 Hollywood Rd, Central, **T** 2868 1316. *2100-0330 Mon-Thu 2100-0500 Fri-Sat. Map 2, F6, p248 See also p213*

Rice Bar, G/F 33 Jervois St, Central, **T** 2851 4800. *1830-0100 Sun-Thu, 1830-0200, Fri 2000-0300 Sat. HH 1830-2100. Map 2, C3, p248 See also p213*

Tower Club, 20-22 D'Aguilar St, Central, **T** 2525 6118. *HH 1800-2100. Map 2, G6/7, p248 See also p213*

Works, 1/F 30-32 Wyndham St, Central, **T** 2868 6102. *1900-0200. HH 1900-2100. Map 2, G6, p248 See also p213*

Admiralty and Wan Chai

Bars

Klong Bar and Grill, G/F The Broadway, 54-62 Lockhart Rd, Wan Chai, **T** 2217 8330. *1500-0300. HH 1700-2100. Map 3, F6, p250* The sumptuous dark wooden bar, round tables and a huge photo of a Bangkok canal market (klong) set the tone. With a good range of Thai drinks (Mekong whisky) and cocktails, it serves satay, ribs and spring rolls all night, and upstairs are a small dance floor, jenga sets, pool table and poles for wannabe pole dancers. The DJ plays mainstream dance music, with more laid-back ambient sounds after midnight. Free vodka for women on Wednesday nights.

one-fifth, 1/F Starcrest, 9 Star St, Wan Chai, **T** 2520 2515. *Corner of Wing Fung St. 1800-0100 Mon-Wed, 1800-0200 Thu, 1800-0300 Fri, 2000-0300 Sat. HH 1800-2100. Map 3, G4, p250* Tricky to find, but a stylish lounge bar with deep-chocolate carpets and dark furnishings. Sophisticated Japanese snacks like sushi platters come from next-door Kokage (p141), and the menu boasts classic cocktails, cigars and champagnes. Music is mainly funk and soul, dress is smart casual.

The Groovy Mule, 37-39 Lockhart Rd, Wan Chai, **T** 2527 2077. *HH 1200-2200. Map 3, F6, p250* A small bar perched on the corner of Lockhart Road and Penwick St, the main attraction here is that the huge doors open onto the delights of Wan Chai, perfect for a people-watching, cooling beer on a hot day. Popular with older expats.

Clubs

Club ING, 4/F Renaissance Harbour View Hotel, 1 Harbour Rd, Wan Chai, **T** 2824 0523. *1700-0400 Mon-Fri, 1730-0400 Sat. Map 3, C9, p251* A glitzy, funky place for a dance, attracting a good mix of people especially trendy Chinese. Assorted DJ nights, free entry for women and men pay around $100 before 2300, with free drinks for women on Thursday. Two separate rooms with different atmosphere with karaoke upstairs. Smart casual dress.

JJs, G/F Grand Hyatt Hong Kong, 1 Harbour Rd, Wan Chai, **T** 2588 1234. *1800-0200 Mon-Thu, 1800-0300 Fri, 1900-0400 Sat. HH 1800-2030 Mon-Fri. Map 3, C9, p251* A huge club and long-standing favourite for years, it has private lounge areas, a small music room with North American R&B bands, live music, *daily from 2200*, salsa night is on Tuesday, and there's free champagne for ladies on Thursdays. Dinner and snacks available. Smart casual dress.

Strawberry Café Disco, 48 Hennessy Rd, Wan Chai, **T** 2866 1031. *2000-late. Map 3, F6, p250* A tacky club where anything goes, with a mix of drunken expats, just clocked-off hostesses and anyone else desperate enough for a cheap late night beer and a dance. The sort of place to end the night, rather than start it, but can be fun.

Causeway Bay and Happy Valley

Bars

Alfred's on the Corner, 14 Yuen Yuen St, Happy Valley, **T** 2575 3181. *1800-0200. Map 1, D4, p247* Cosy bar in an alleyway which has always been popular for its great selection of wines, and bar snacks. The decor is enhanced by plenty of plants and flowers.

Green Spot, 1/F 1 Wong Nai Chung Rd, Happy Valley, **T** 2836 0009. *1830-0300 Sun-Thu, 1830-0400 Fri-Sat. Map 1, D4, p247* The place for hanging out, people watching and expensive drinks – very stylish minimalist décor which seems to attract the local celebs. A place to celebrate the big win at the races.

Tsim Sha Tsui

Bars

Biergarten, 5 Hanoi Rd, Tsim Sha Tsui, **T** 2721 2302. *1200-0200. HH 1600-2100. Map 5, I6, p255* The place for beer lovers, with two draught German beers and other bottled varieties, plus German food like smoked pork sausages with mashed potatoes and sauerkraut.

Delaney's, B/F Mary Building, 71-77 Peking Rd, Tsim Sha Tsui, **T** 2301 3980. *0900-0200. HH 1700-2100. Map 5, J4, p255* A good-natured noisy pub with live music on Wed and Fri, plus DJ nights, quizzes, good international sport on TV and traditional Irish food, including tiramisu, made with Irish whiskey.

Felix, 28/F The Peninsula Hotel, Salisbury Rd, Tsim Sha Tsui, **T** 2315 3188. *1800-0200. Map 5, K4, p255 See also p146* If a meal here is beyond your means (one of the most expensive restaurants in town) then settle down and sip a cocktail in the Phillipe Starck-designed interior which oozes class, and gaze at the harbour view at your leisure.

Ned Kelly's Last Stand, 11A Ashley Rd, Tsim Sha Tsui. *1130-0200. HH 1130-2100. Map 5, I3, p255* No-nonsense Aussie pub with live Dixieland jazz after 2100, not-so-healthy meaty food and naturally attracting foreign tourists and workers.

New Wally Matt Lounge, G/F 5A Humphrey's Ave, Tsim Sha Tsui, **T** 2721 2568, enquiry@wallymatt.com *1700-0400. HH 1700-2200. Map 5, H5, p255 See also p212*

PJ Murphy's Irish Pub, B/F Imperial Hotel, 32 Nathan Rd, Tsim Sha Tsui, **T** 2782 3383. *1200-0200. HH 1700-2000. Map 5, J4, p255* Large choice of beers and stouts and well-known for its Irish rock oysters, fresh on the half-shell or deep-fried, and beef and Guinness boxty.

Someplace Else, B/F Sheraton Hong Kong Hotel, 20 Nathan Rd, Tsim Sha Tsui, **T** 2721 6151. *1200-0130 Sun-Thu, 1200-0230 Fri-Sat. HH 1700-2000. Map 5, J5, p255* Best known for its cocktails and live jazz from the in-house band, it has tables and wooden booths over two floors.

Wally Matt Bar and Lounge, G/F 3 Granville Circuit, Tsim Sha Tsui, **T** 2367-6874, wm@wallymatt.com.hk *1700-0400. Map 5, G6, p255 See also p213*

Lantau

Bars

Hippo, G/F Grand View Mansion, 11 Mui Wo Ferry Pier Rd, Mui Wo, **T** 2984 9876. *1200-2400, HH 1600-2200 Mon-Fri, all day Sat and Sun.* Expat-flavoured pub complete with English draught beers, European football, bangers and mash and Sunday roast. Internet access (\$20/30 mins) and second-hand books. Located in a small courtyard near the ferry pier.

China Bear, G/F Mui Wo Centre, Mui Wo, **T** 2984 7360. *1000-0100. HH 1600-2200 Mon-Fri, 1700-2000 Sat.* Longstanding favourite with local expats, tourists and day trippers from Hong Kong, with pool tables and TV beaming European football. So-so pub food, *1000-2200*, includes burgers, steak and sandwiches.

Macau

Bars

The Embassy Bar, Mandarin Oriental Hotel, 956-1110 Av da Amizade, **T** 793 3830. *1700-0130*. A plush venue popular with expats, and good for a relaxing evening.

Clubs

DD Disco, Av Inf da Henrique, Silo Sintra, **T** 711 800. *2230-0700*. A pretty down-to-earth place attracting a fun-loving, mixed crowd with a Thai band performing popular hits. For night birds!

Jazz Club, Cafeteria Artsy, Macau Cultural Center, **T** 797 7755. *Fri and Sat 2100-0300*. New venue for an old established club, with live jazz in an informal atmosphere.

Club Rukas, 85 Rua Fransisco H Fernandes, **T** 751 799. A huge, packed and lively bar popular with young Chinese, with a karaoke lounge and the cheapest beer in town.

Check out...

WWW...

100 travel guides, 100s of destinations,
5 continents
and 1 Footprint...

www.footprintbooks.com

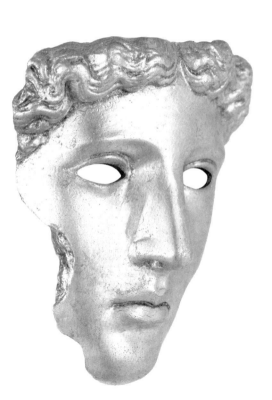

Hong Kong has good grounds for claiming to be the events capital of Asia with a wide variety of Chinese and western arts and cultural events throughout the year. The **Hong Kong Arts Festival** (Feb-Mar) is three weeks of entertainment ranging from international orchestras and classical ballet, to Shakespeare translated into Cantonese. The two-week **International Film Festival** in April covers obscure to mainstream to archival and reflects a growing respect for Hong Kong cinema prompted by the success of Cannes award-winning *In the Mood for Love* and Ang Lee's superb *Crouching Tiger Hidden Dragon*. Music ranges from concerts of **Cantopop heart-throbs**, the occasional appearance from **classic crooners** in the Cliff Richard and Elton John mould, and major acts like the Rolling Stones, to **Cantonese opera** and Carmen, with the Hong Kong Philharmonic Orchestra also playing regularly. There is little variety in the alternative **independent music** scene; live music in bars tends to be limited to hotel "house" bands performing covers of well-known pop anthems and the occasional decent jazz artist in a couple of clubs around Lan Kwai Fong.

Information on all events can be obtained in the *South China Morning Post*, *HK Magazine* and *BC Magazine*. Tickets for major events can be bought through: **URBTIX**, **T** 2734 9011; overseas bookings **T** +852 2734 9001; **Ticketek T** 3128 8288; **Ticketnet T** 2312 9991; **Cityline T** 2111 5333.

Cinema

Most English-language films shown in Hong Kong cinemas are predictable Hollywood blockbusters, with romance and action being the most popular. The best bet for anything off that well-worn route is during the excellent **International Film Festival** (see p182) at the new **Hong Kong Film Archive** (see p59) and the occasional gem at the Cine Art House, AMC Festival Walk and the Arts Centre. There are many cinemas around town, costing between $50-$60 a ticket, with full listings and reviews in newspapers, HK and BC magazines.

That said, the local film industry is a fascinating one if you like action, producing two of the world's big names in **Bruce Lee** and **Jackie Chan**. Lee can be credited with bringing the martial arts film – especially kung fu – and Hong Kong cinema to international prominence, while Chan is still a Hollywood icon, usually playing the humble comic nice guy overcoming the bad guy, and performing his own stunts in spectacular fashion. Local films can be fun, but check that there are English subtitles.

The Hong Kong film industry, the third biggest in the world in terms of output, has always been respected for its action and martial arts, especially with recent directors like **John Woo**. But it reached new heights with **Ang Lee**'s *Crouching Tiger Hidden Dragon* winning four Oscars in 2001, starring Michelle Yeoh and Chow Yun-fat, a combination of mythical heroism in ancient China, bandits, romance and magical fight scenes, and was the most successful foreign language film ever.

Local Cinemas

AMC Festival Walk, UG/F, 88 Tat Chee Ave, Kowloon Tong, **T** 2265 8595 (booking) **T** 2265 8545 (info). Large multiplex with 11 screens in smart shopping centre. Mainly US films, some Cantonese plus non-English and non-mainstream.

Cine-Art House, 30 Harbour Rd, Sun Hung Kai Centre, Wan Chai, **T** 2827 4820. A small venue and the best art-house cinema in this part of town with foreign or older films.

Film Archive Cinema, 50 Lei King Rd, Sai Wan Ho, **T** 2739 2139, www.filmarchive.gov.hk The new archive has a wonderful cinema showing innovative local, independent and old foreign films. A bit of a trek to get to, but worth stopping by.

Golden Gateway, 25 Canton Rd, Tsim Sha Tsui, **T** 2956 2471. A six-screen cinema, all mainstream Hollywood stuff.

Grand Ocean, 3 Canton Rd, Tsim Sha Tsui, **T** 2377 2100. A tiny venue with one screen.

Lim Por Yen Film Theatre, Hong Kong Arts Centre, 2 Harbour Rd, Wan Chai, **T** 2582 0200. Hong Kong's first art-house cinema regularly shows archival, independent and foreign films from around the world, and holds regular festivals.

Silvercord Cinema, G/F Silvercord Centre, 30 Canton Rd, Tsim Sha Tsui, **T** 2736 6218. Part of the Broadway group. Three screens with a mix of new Chinese and western films.

UA Pacific Place, G/F Level 1 Pacific Pl, 88 Queensway, Admiralty, **T** 2869 0322. Adjacent to the shopping centre and the most accessible to Central.

Music

The best-loved genre of music by far is Cantopop (see box p172), but if that is hard to handle then there are many choices of classical with the Hong Kong Philharmonic, Chinese classical, Chinese opera, contemporary music and jazz, played in a variety of venues (see p174). Western pop and rock caters to a very mainstream market and there are no real surprises. Jazz is limited to a handful of venues around Central, the occasional big star performing at one of the Cultural Centres. For more avant-garde stuff, check the Fringe Club.

Cantonese Opera is an acquired taste but is definitely a very different musical experience and a highly respected art form dating back to the late 12th century, which combines heroic tales, action, Chinese legends, music and drama. Performances are often over three hours long and are lost on the novice if there are no surtitles, although from a purely visual spectacle its incredible costumes and make-up are definitely entertaining. The **Sun Beam Cinema** (see p58) is one of the only traditional venues of pure Cantonese Opera, and one of the most authentic experiences of its traditional roots is at **Temple Street Night Market** (see p75). Other forms of Chinese opera, like Peking and Sichuan, can be seen at various Cultural Centres and are more likely to have surtitles.

Music organizations

Cantonese Opera Appreciation Tour, Hong Kong Heritage Museum 1 Man Lam Rd, Sha Tin, registration **T** 2508 1234. *1430-1545 Sat*. This tour around the museum's section on Cantonese Opera is a great introduction before going to a performance, offering something of an insight into an otherwise often baffling experience.

! In a recent survey of people admired by Hong Kong teenagers, nine out of the top 10 were Cantopop stars. The exception was God, who was ninth.

▶ Cantopop – the music machine

Hong Kong's own brand of pop music, known as Cantopop, has changed little over the years, and although outsiders see it as pretty dire and predictable, it is one of the most significant entertainment markets in Hong Kong and an industry worth billions of dollars every year. What it lacks in musical freedom and original expression, it adequately makes up for in feel-good ballads and sugary sentiment, and fits in perfectly to a well-packaged product of style over substance. Stars have been carefully selected and are always pretty (male and female), their appearance and often names changed to suit a hungry audience.

Developing in the late 60s and early 70s following a demand from Hong Kong audiences for pop music in their own language, the first major Cantopop stars emerged in the 80s, with fan wars between followers of **Alan Tam** (lead singer of The Wynners) and **Leslie Cheung**. Heart-throbs for thousands of obsessive teenage girls, they both subsequently retreated from the scene when the fan fighting became too intense.

They both made comebacks in the 1990s but were overshadowed by The Four Heavenly Kings: **Jacky Cheung** (also referred to as the God of Songs); **Andy Lau** (cute actor, once making nine films simultaneously and the first Asian face of Pepsi); **Leon Lai** (Heavenly King of Fan Support); and **Aaron Kwok** (Heavenly King of Dance). Not to be outdone by the pretty boys, the best-known female stars are **Sammi Cheng**, (30 albums by the time she was 29 and a flourishing film career) and **Faye Wong** (also an actress, known to be moody and difficult).

But the days of this heavenly foursome are obviously numbered and hot on their trail is the new group known as the Four Young Kings of Cantopop: Nicholas Tse, Leo Koo, Daniel Chan and Stephen Fung.

Hong Kong Philharmonic Orchestra, 8/F Administative Building, HK Cultural Centre, Tsim Sha Tsui, **T** 2721 2030, www.hkpo.com *0900-1815 Mon-Fri, 0900-1300 Sat*. Going strong since 1895 with 89 members, this is the city's oldest and largest orchestra and has performed with stars like Isaac Stern, Yo-Yo Ma and Vladimir Ashkenazy. Music ranges from Bach and Bruckner to contemporary Asian and western music.

Hong Kong Chinese Orchestra, www.hkco.org Founded in 1977, this is Hong Kong's only professional Chinese orchestra and does a lot to promote Chinese music and culture with a combination of traditional modernized Chinese and western instruments.

Hong Kong Sinfonietta, **T** 2836 3336, www.hksinfonietta.org Since 1990, the Hong Kong Sinfonietta has promoted lesser-heard works by Chinese composers, and collaborated with Pavarotti, the Kirov and Bolshoi ballet companies.

Dance

The dance scene ranges between classical ballet from the Hong Kong Ballet to avant-garde movement, dance and drama from City Contemporary Dance Company. See also Venues listings below.

Hong Kong Ballet, **T** 2573 7398, www.hkballet.com One of the best classical ballet companies in Asia, ably led by Stephen Jefferies. The troupe has over 40 dancers mainly from Hong Kong and Asia. Recent performances include favourites like *Coppelia*, *Turandot* and *Swan Lake*, and the distinctly Asian style of *The Last Emperor*.

City Contemporary Dance Company, **T** 2326 8597, www.ccdc.com.hk A promoter of predominantly Chinese-influenced modern dance and contemporary culture, the company bills itself as "the artistic soul of contemporary Hong Kong".

Zuni Icosahedron, www.zuni.org.hk Hard to put into one category, Zuni is probably the best-known avant-garde group in Hong Kong, combining dance, drama, movement, music and multi-media installations in their performances, which are usually in Cantonese (if indeed there is any speech).

Venues

Blue Door, 5/F 37 Cochrane St, Central, **T** 2858 6555. *Fri-Sat. Map 2, E5, p248* One of the few jazz venues in town with live bands on Fri and Sat only. Relaxed informal setting typical performers might be Blaine Whittaker Quartet or Rickard Malsten Group.

Cultural Centre, 10 Salisbury Rd, Tsim Sha Tsui, **T** 2734 2010, 2734 2848, www.hkculturalcentre.gov.hk *MTR: Tsim Sha Tsui. (See p70.) Map 5, K3, p255 See also p70* One of Hong Kong's largest venues for concerts and theatre, its hundreds of annual events include orchestral concerts, ballet, Chinese opera and pop, and it is a significant venue in the Hong Kong Arts Festival.

Fringe Club, 2 Lower Albert Rd, Central, **T** 2521 7251, www.hkfringeclub.com *MTR: Central. Map 2, G6, p248 See p39*

Hong Kong Academy of Performing Arts, 1 Gloucester Rd, Wan Chai, **T** 2584 8500, www.hkapa.edu *Map 3, D6, p250* Hosting opera, theatre and musicals and has an Open-Air Theatre for large-scale events set in attractive gardens. It often has free concerts in afternoons and early evenings given by students of the Academy.

Hong Kong Arts Centre 2 Harbour Rd, Wan Chai, **T** 2582 0200, www.hkac.org.hk *Map 3, D6, p250* A great independent venue for the arts, including the 439-seater Shouson Theatre which hosts local theatre groups especially the Hong Kong Repertory Theatre.

Hong Kong City Hall, 7 Edinburgh Pl, Central, **T** 2921 2840,
www.cityhall.gov.hk *Map 2, F11, p249* *See p38* The first
multi-purpose cultural community centre in Hong Kong.

Hong Kong Coliseum, 9 Cheong Wan Rd, Hung Hom, Kowloon,
T 2355 7234. The 12,500-seat Coliseum is a well-equipped,
multi-purpose indoor stadium hosting large-scale events,
especially pop and rock concerts.

Hong Kong Convention and Exhibition Centre, 1 Expo Dr,
Wan Chai, **T** 2582 8888, www.hkcec.com *MTR: Wan Chai. Map 3,
C8, p251* *See p53* Oozing out from Wan Chai's waterfront, this
swathe of glass and sweeping sails is one of Asia's largest
convention centres but also has two theatres.

Ko Shan Theatre Ko Shan Rd Park, Hung Hom, Kowloon,
T 2740 9222. *0900-2300, box office 1000-1830. MTR: Mongkok exit
B2, then minibus #27M.* The former amphitheatre was demolished
and reopened in 1996 with an air-conditioned foyer block, housing
a theatre, rehearsal facilities and exhibition space.

Music Room Live, 2/F California Entertainment Building, 34-36
D'Aguilar St, Central, **T** 2845 8477. *1930-late. MTR: Central. Map 2,
F7, p248* Previously the Jazz Club and Bar, the newly formed venue
stages big names in international blues and jazz, as well as salsa,
Cuban and R&B.

Queen Elizabeth Stadium, 18 Oi Kwan Rd, Wan Chai, **T** 2591
1346. *Box office 1000-1830. MTR: Wan Chai. Map 4, H1, p252*
Inaugurated on 27 August 1980, the close proximity between the
stage and the spectator grandstand makes it ideal for big rock gigs.

Sha Tin Town Hall, 1 Yuen Wo Rd, Sha Tin, **T** 2694 2511. *KCR: Sha
Tin. Map 6, p256* One of Hong Kong's best performing arts venues

and at the heart of the cultural activities in the eastern New Territories. Its medium-scale capacity is a venue for dance, drama and music, mainly staging Chinese opera.

Sheung Wan Civic Centre, 4/F-7/F 345 Queen's Rd Central, Sheung Wan, **T** 2853 2668. *MTR: Sheung Wan.* *Map 1, C2, p247* A community arts centre with a combination of performing, rehearsal, lecture and exhibition facilities and an URBTIX outlet.

Sai Wan Ho Civic Centre, G/F 111 Shau Kei Wan Rd, Sai Wan Ho, **T** 2568 5998. *MTR: Sai Wan Ho.* *Map 2, D6, p248* The community arts centre contains venues for performance, film, lectures, meetings, exhibitions, and a 471-seat theatre showing a variety of Cantonese opera, Chinese drama and dance.

Tsuen Wan Town Hall, 72 Tai Ho Rd, Tsuen Wan, **T** 2414 0144, booking **T** 2493 7463, twth@lcsd.gov.hk *MTR: Tsuen Wan.* *Map 6, p256* The 1424-seater auditorium has good acoustics and has hosted orchestras and soloists from around the world.

Every modern city in the world has its fare share of festivals centred around films, arts, shopping and music. But, interspersed with such commercial and sophisticated events, the beauty of Hong Kong is in the ability to experience a traditional culture that is otherwise hard to see. The larger celebrations, like **Chinese New Year** or **Dragon Boat Races**, are difficult to miss but it is as culturally insightful to track down festivities in remote areas. It's also a wonderful way of learning about a deep cultural love of legends, superstition and tradition, which would otherwise be hard to picture when looking at all those cheap plastic watches. The three-week **Arts Festival** in February is one of the best in Asia, staging international acts of jazz, classical music, ballet and theatre, and the **International Film Festival** in April gives Hong Kong audiences a rare chance to see old classics or obscure films. The **Chinese Arts Festival** is a promotion of Chinese culture and history, while at the other end of the scale is the mammoth **Hong Kong Rugby Sevens**, an international sporting and drinking fest.

⭐ Funky festivals

Best

- **Dragon Boat Festival** Carved dragons' heads on boats, drummers and frantic paddlers, p183.
- **Chinese New Year** The all-night flower market in Victoria Park, pack-out temples and a huge parade, below.
- **Cheung Chau Bun Festival** Parades, temple celebrations, children dressed as dolls – and buns, p105.
- **Monkey God Festival** Possessed medium running over hot coals, p184.
- **Mid Autumn (Mooncake) Festival** Late evening in the parks the lanterns under the harvest moon, p184.

January

Chinese New Year (Jan or Feb) Hong Kong claims to be the world capital for these celebrations. Falling between mid-Jan and mid-Feb, the first day of the first moon marks the start of Lunar New Year, the biggest festival in the Chinese culture. Festivities include a parade with floats between Admiralty and Wan Chai, a huge firework display over Victoria Harbour, the all-night flower market in Victoria Park, skyscrapers lit up and decorated even more than usual, and temples chock-full of worshippers. Lai See packets (small red envelopes containing money) are also handed out to family and friends. It is a time for visiting family and going to temple, and most shops, restaurants and museums are closed for at least two days.

Birthday of Che Kung (Jan or Feb – 2nd or 3rd day of Lunar New Year) This Sung Dynasty general became immortal and elevated to Taoist deity after he saved the people of Sha Tin from a plague. His temple, near the racecourse, is especially popular on his birthday with local gamblers who pop in on their way to the track, in order to get their fortunes told to see which horse will be lucky.

Festivals and events

Spring Lantern Festival (Jan or Feb) Sometimes referred to as Chinese Valentine's Day, this comes 15 days into the Chinese New Year and marks the end of the celebrations with colourful lanterns in traditional design lighting up markets, houses, parks and restaurants.

February

Hong Kong Arts Festival (mid-Feb to early Mar) Hong Kong Arts Festival Society, 12/F Hong Kong Arts Centre, 2 Harbour Rd, Wan Chai, **T** 2824 3555, www.hk.artsfestival.org Various venues. A major international arts festival and the premier arts event in the Asia-Pacific region, this annual festival puts on international acts, plus those from China and Hong Kong. Entertainment throughout the three weeks includes opera, western classical music, jazz, contemporary dance, ballet and theatre in various venues.

Nosso Senhor dos Passos (Procession of Holy Christ) (Feb/Mar) An image of Christ carrying the Cross is taken in solemn procession from St Augustine's Church to the Cathedral in Macau for a night vigil. It is then returned through the city via the stations of the Cross, accompanied by a magenta-robed escort and crowds of people.

March

Qing Ming Festival (Mar/Apr) On this day most of Hong Kong flocks up to the burial areas in the New Territories for grave sweeping, to pay respect to their ancestors by cleaning the gravestones, clearing weeds and making offerings of wine and fruit. The roads, and all public transport, to these areas are congested and often delayed, so it is a difficult time for visitors to travel here.

Hong Kong Rugby Sevens (last weekend of Mar) (National Stadium) Hong Kong Rugby Football Union, Rm 2001, Sports House, 1 Stadium Path, So Kon Po, Causeway Bay, **T** 2504 8311, www.hksevens.com.hk Recognized as being the premier leg of the World Rugby 7s series, this is Hong Kong's biggest sporting event of the year and notorious for being one solid three-day party. **Hong Kong Rugby Tens** (Hong Kong Football Club) Hong Kong Rugby Football Union. With 24 teams from around the world, this prestigious three-day tournament is immediately before the Sevens, the curtain raiser for the bigger event. **Women's Rugby Sevens** Hong Kong Rugby Football Union. This tournament has now been established as the only one of its kind in this region; an internationally recognized rugby tournament for women.

Hong Kong Derby (Mid-Mar) Royal Hong Kong Jockey Club, 1 Sports Rd, Happy Valley, Sha Tin, **T** 2966 8111, www.hongkong jockeyclub.com One of the biggest races of the season with over $14m prize money on offer, more than the Epsom, Irish or French derbies, with international thoroughbreds.

Flower Show (2nd week Mar) Victoria Park, Causeway Bay, **T** 2723 6232, www.lcsd.gov.hk Inspiration to buy some gardening gloves: this 10-day festival spread over the park has extravagant floral displays from Hong Kong, China and around the world, with over 3,000 plants in the competition plus around 75 stalls selling horticultural products.

Macau Arts Festival www.icm.gov.mo Organized by the Cultural Institute, this is a showcase for most of Macau's cultural associations, in a programme which includes a wide variety of music, dance, exhibitions, Chinese opera and theatre at different venues.

April

Birthday of Tin Hau, also **A-Ma** in Macau (April or May) Tin Hau, the Taoist goddess of the sea and patron saint of seafarers, is one of Hong Kong's (and Macau's) most revered gods and there are temples in her honour throughout the territory. During the festival, fishing boats decorated with flags and banners sail to their nearest temple and on land there are lion dances and parades.

International Film Festival (2nd and 3rd week Apr) 22/F 181 Queen's Rd Central, **T** 2970 3300, www.hkiff.org.hk *0900-1730 Mon-Fri, 0900-1200 Sat*. This two-week festival showcases everything from current Palm D'Or and Academy Award winners to obscure old films from around the world. There is a special emphasis on independent film-makers and of course many Asian films.

Le French May Festival of Arts (last week Apr) (Assorted venues.) www.frenchmay.com Tickets: www.urbtix.gov.hk The grandest French festival in Asia includes classical and contemporary French arts. It is a well-respected cultural event over six weeks and includes ballet, architecture, photography, jazz, visual arts and mime.

Buddha's Birthday (Apr/May) Worshippers bathe Buddha's statue and there are celebrations around the major monasteries and temples, especially Po Lin (Lantau) and Miu Fat (Tuen Mun) Monasteries.

Tam Kung's Birthday (Apr/May) Celebrating another patron of the sea at the Tam Kung temple in Shau Kei Wan (built in 1905), seafarers pray for safety and good luck on their travels.

May

Cheung Chau Bun Festival (See p105).

Procession of Our Lady of Fatima (13 May) (Macau) An annual procession of devotees, from Santo Domingo's Church to the Penha Chapel, where an open-air mass is said, to commemorate the miracle of Fatima in Portugal in 1917.

Dragon Boat Festival Stanley Residents' Association, 96 Stanley Main St, **T** 2813 0564, www.dragonboat.org.hk Also known as Tuen Ng festival, this commemorates the death of a Chinese national hero, Qu Yuan, who drowned himself in Mi Lo River over 2000 years ago to protest against corrupt rulers. Villagers beat drums to scare away the fish and stop his body being eaten. Since 1975 this has been celebrated with dragon boat races, including over 100 teams from all over the world. Each boat has 20-22 paddlers, a carved dragon's head at the bow, with one person beating a huge drum.

July

Kwan Tai's Birthday Kwan Tai is the god of war, patron of the Hong Kong police and gangsters, who lived between AD 220-265.

August

Feast of Hungry Ghosts (Yue Laan) (Aug/Sep) During this month, ghosts are supposed to roam the earth so Chinese people tend to avoid late nights to dodge the spirits, and some burn paper money and make offerings at the roadside to appease the restless ghosts. It is also a popular time for Chinese opera performances.

Feast of Maidens (Seven Sisters) Dedicated to girls and young lovers, the origins of this festival go back around 1500 years into the mists of Chinese folklore and the legend of a maiden weaver who was fixed her up by her father with a cow-herder. However, she neglected her weaving, provoking him to restrict her 'wifely duties' to just the seventh day of the seventh moon. To mark the occasion, young women make offerings, burn incense and gather around Lover's Rock on Bowen Road in Wan Chai.

Monkey God Festival (Sep/Oct)   A mischievous god originating from a novel during the Ming Dynasty (1368-1644), Monkey was also immortalized in a BBC2 series back in the 1970s. An outcast from Taoist heaven, he gained Buddhist immortality by escorting Tang Gan Zang on his pilgrimage to the West. In Sau Mau Ping in Kowloon, a shanty town temple recreates the ordeals by fire and stabbing which the Monkey God suffered when other gods tried to kill him. These are performed by a possessed medium who runs over hot coals and climbs a ladder of knives.

Chung Yeung (Feast of Ancestors) (Sep or Oct)   Also known as Autumn remembrance, respect of ancestors is crucial to this festival, similar to Ching Ming when people go to their ancestor's graves to clean them. Because of a legend, it is a popular day for hiking, especially to high altitudes.

Mid Autumn (Mooncake) Festival (Sep or Oct)   The festival commemorates a 14th-century uprising against the Mongols, when rebels wrote the call to revolt on pieces of paper that they hid inside cakes to smuggle to their compatriots. During this time, piles of cakes are sold outside bakeries, stuffed with a mixture of ground lotus, egg yolk and bean paste, and kids carry paper lanterns in the shape of dragons or rockets and light them from a high peak, while gazing at the huge autumn moon. The best place to be during this festival is in a public park in the late evening.

International Fireworks Display Contest (Macau) (Every Sunday in Sep)   The largest event of its kind in the world, this contest sees participants flying in from all over the world to light up the sky with pyrotechnic wizardry, with displays at 2100 and 2200 over Sai Van Lake.

October

Hong Kong Chinese Arts Festival (mid Oct-mid Nov)
www.discoverhongkong.com For one month, this biennial (2003,
2005 etc) presents the best arts and culture from China, Taiwan
and Hong Kong, including stage, exhibitions and seminars, with
the aim of promoting understanding and appreciation of Chinese
culture and history. Events are held at various locations.

Macau International Music Festival This brings together
orchestras, choirs and musicians from around the world, with a
combination of western, Chinese classical and contemporary
music, usually with an opera as the finale. Venues range from
baroque churches, Chinese pavilions and the Cultural Centre.

Spirals of incense
A feature of every Chinese temple, symbolising food for the spirits.

Omega Hong Kong Open Golf Championships (Nov/Dec)
Hong Kong Golf Association, Rm 2003, Sports House, 1 Stadium
Path, So Kon Po, Causeway Bay, **T** 2504 8659, Hkgolf@hkga.com
The longest-running professional sports event in Hong Kong.

Macau Grand Prix (mid-Nov) Macau Grand Prix Committee, 207
Av da Amizade, Edif do Grande Premio, Macau, **T** (853) 796 2268,
www.macau.grandprix.gov.mo One of the Formula 3 events to
travel through the picturesque city streets. Motorcycle races are also
held during the week, and not surprisingly this is Macau's busiest
time – advanced booking for travel and accommodation is essential.

December

Hong Kong WinterFest www.discoverhongkong.com Seasonal
celebrations including the switching on of the Christmas lights, a City
of Life street carnival, themed food districts and other festive events.

International Races (Mid-Dec) (Sha Tin) Royal Hong Kong
Jockey Club, 1 Sports Rd, Happy Valley, **T** 2966 8111,
www.hongkongjockeyclub.com One of the biggest race meetings
of the year, with four international Group 1 events making up the
first leg of the World Series Racing Championships.

Dong Zhi (Winter Solstice) (Dec 21) The second-most
important festival after Chinese New Year. Families celebrate the
coming of winter and farmers and fishermen gather food in
preparation for the coming cold season. It is believed that this is
the strongest time of yin (symbolizing dark and cold) but it also
signifies a turning point as it gives way to yang (light and warm).

Consumerism is a mammoth part of life here so, not surprisingly, shopping still plays an important part of most visitors' trips to Hong Kong, even though there may not be the great bargains of previous years. Whether seeking out the newest digital cameras on **Stanley Street**, rummaging through piles of knock-off designer gear in **Wan Chai**, or wandering through **Temple Street** or **Stanley Markets** for tacky souvenirs, the selection and value is pretty good. Prices are usually displayed in markets, although haggling is de rigeur especially if buying more than one of any item, so keep it good-natured and realistic for greater success. Fashionistas should head for the glossy shopping malls in **Central** and **Admiralty**, with D&G, Prada and Gucci galore, and if the wallet can't stretch that far, the designer outlets stores have vastly reduced prices and decent labels even find there way to the bargain bin in chaotic stores around Wan Chai, Causeway Bay and Tsim Sha Tsui. Reputable camera and video shops are clustered around Stanley Street, so avoid Tsim Sha Tsui, and for a huge range of computers try Botanical in **Causeway Bay**.

Hollywood Road is the best for contemporary Asian art, antiques, curios and furniture, including many of the galleries listed in the Galleries and Museums section, and **Wyndham Street** has carpet shops with imports from India, China, Iran and Pakistan. Most stores in Central and Western are open between 1000-1900; Wan Chai, Causeway Bay, Tsim Sha Tsui and Mongkok 1000-2200.

Arts, crafts and antiques

Chinese Arts and Crafts, China Resources Bldg, 26 Harbour Rd, Wan Chai, **T** 2827 6667. *1030-1930. Map 3, D9, p251* Asia Standard Tower, 59 Queen's Rd C, Central, **T** 2901 0338. *1030-1930. Map 2, E7, p248* Star House, 3 Salisbury Rd, Tsim Sha Tsui, **T** 2735 4061. *1000-2130. Map 5, K2, p255* Huge stores good for stocking up on gifts. Sells Chinese traditional arts, antiques and handicrafts.

The Fine Arts Studio, 203A Hollywood Rd, Central, **T** 2544 6898. *1100-1800 Tue-Sun. Map 2, C23, p248* Tiny shop crammed with Mao memorabilia, old Hong Kong postcards, communist China posters and Bruce Lee posters, plus antique birdcages and stamps.

MinGei Antiques, 50 Wyndham St, Central, **T** 2524 5518. *1000-1900. Map 2, G6, p248* Antique birdcages and wooden furniture from the Qing and Mong dynasties.

The Red Lantern Shop, G03, Silver Plaza, Mui Wo, Lantau, **T** 2984 0099. *Map 6, p256* Small friendly English/Chinese- owned store with good-value imported furniture and antiques from China. Will ship stuff back to your home if the sideboard doesn't fit in your suitcase.

Saikung Gallery, 53 Sai Kung Villa, Fuk Man Rd, Sai Kung, **T** 2791 5886. *1030-2000. Map 6, p256* Small selection of antiques and Chinese furniture.

▶ Tricks and scams

Unsuspecting shoppers, especially of electronic items, are sometimes the victims of various scams that can lead to misery when they get their goods home and find an inferior or incomplete model. 'Bait and Switch' is the most common trick, where vendors put great items in the window then switch the model for an inferior one. This is most common along the Golden Mile, with its wall-to-wall camera and electronic stores. Also some dealers are not authorized to sell certain imported goods, especially those coming from China, so warranties are often invalid. Likewise gems, jewellery and antiques can often be fakes (good stores will give you a certificate of authenticity).

The best way to sift the dodgy dealers from the reputable retailers is to take note of the Quality Tourism Services (QTS), awarded by the Hong Kong Tourism Board to shops and restaurants (indicated by a sticker on their door or on advertisements in the press). These establishments should provide high quality products and services. Always insist on a full warranty (worldwide) for electronic goods, or a certificate of authenticity on antiques and gems, and ensure that the product is compatible with the voltage system etc back home.

For queries regarding a store or product: **Consumer Council Complaints and Advice Hotline** T 2929 2222. **Consumer Council Advice Centre**: G/F Harbour Bldg, 38 Pier Rd, Central, T 2921 6228.

Wai Tat Industries Shop, 32-37, Peak Galleria, The Peak, **T** 2367 0878. *1000-2200. Map 1, D2, p247* Large store with Chinese arts and crafts of all price ranges; good for souvenirs.

Yue Hwa Chinese Products Emporium, 54-64 and 143-161 Nathan Rd, Tsim Sha Tsui, **T** 2368 9165. *0930-2130 and 1000-2200 respectively. Map 5, E4, p254* 39 Queen's Rd, Central, **T** 2522 2333.

1000-1930. Map 2, E7, p249 1 Kowloon Park Dr, Kowloon, **T** 2317 5333. *0930-2200.* A huge, well laid-out store selling Chinese goods, from tins of tea to life-size bronze warriors, plus jade and wooden carved ornaments, silk clothes and Chinese medicine.

Bakeries

Ali-Oli, 11 Sha Tsui Path, Sai Kung, **T** 2792 2655. *0700-1900. Map 6, p256 See also p150* A fabulous range of home-made breads, cakes and pies. One of Hong Kong's finest.

Books

Cosmos Books, 30 Johnston Rd, Wan Chai, **T** 2866 1677. *1000-2000. Map 3, G6, p250* The main store has a good selection of English language books. Also a smaller branch at 96 Nathan Rd, Tsim Sha Tsui, **T** 2367 8699. *1030-2100.*

Dymocks Star Ferry Concourse, Central, **T** 2801 4423. *0800-2230 Mon-Sat, 0900-2200 Sun and public holidays. Map 2, D10, p249* Shops F-G, 2/F Windsor House, 311 Gloucester Rd, Causeway Bay, **T** 2915 7757. *1000-2200. Map 4, D7, p253* Carries a good range of local and foreign guidebooks and maps, plus some of fiction and non-fiction.

Hong Kong Book Centre, B/F On Lok Yuen Building, 25 Des Voeux Rd C, **T** 2523 6895. *Map 2, E8, p249* A huge selection of foreign books and newspapers in a cramped store.

Page One, 2/F Century Sq, 1-13 D'Aguilar St, Central, **T** 2536 0111. *Map 2, F7, p249* Shop LG1 30, Festival Walk, Kowloon Tong, **T** 2778 2808. Shop 3002, Zone A Harbour City, Canton Rd, Tsim Sha Tsui, **T** 2730 6080. *Map 5, I2, p255* Basement One, Times Square, Causeway Bay, **T** 2917 7252. *Map 4, F3, p252 All stores approx*

1100-2200 daily. A good selection of English language fiction and non-fiction. The largest braches are Festival Walk and Times Square, also with comfortable in-store cafés.

Chinese medicine

Good Spring Company, 8 Cochrane St, Central, **T** 2544 3518. *0830-2000 Mon-Sat. Map 2, E6, p248* English speaking doctors, qualified in western and eastern medicine. Consultations for $30, prescriptions from range of medication for around $40-50 per dose.

Chinese tea

Ngan Ki Heung Tea Co, 290 Queen's Rd, Central, **T** 2544 1375. *0930-1900 Mon-Sat, 1400-1900 Sun. Map 2, D2, p248* Opening in 1928 with over 200 types of tea, mainly from Taiwan, this is one of Hong Kong's oldest. Staff can explain the health benefits of each tea, such as helping digestion or reducing high blood pressure. Also sells traditional teapots and cups and books on Chinese tea.

Ying Kee Tea House, 151 Queen's Rd, Central, **T** 2544 3811. *Map 2, D5, p248* Shop G8 28 Hankow Rd, Tsim Sha Tsui, **T** 2721 7300. *Map 5, I4, p255* Even older, trading since 1881, there are several stores around town with fine teas selected mainly from China.

Cigars

Cigar Express, G/F Hyatt Regency, 12 Lock Rd, Tsim Sha Tsui, **T** 2366 2537. *1100-2200. Map 5, I4, p255* 45-47 Cochrane St, Central, **T** 2110 9201. *1100-2300. Map 2, E5, p248* Shop 19, 2/F Peak Galleria, The Peak, **T** 2849 8198. *1000-2100. Map 1, D2, p247* A relatively new trend in Hong Kong, this chain of express outlets gives friendly assistance for the non-aficionado and has a range of mainly Cuban cigars between $20-200 each.

La Tradición Cubana, 54 D'Aguilar St, Central, **T** 2525 7466. *1400-2300 Mon-Thu, 1400-0100 Fri and Sat. Map 2, G6, p248* Opened in 2001, the tiny store has a fine range of Cuban cigars.

Department stores and shopping malls

Beverley Commercial Centre, 87-105 Chatham Rd, Tsim Sha Tsui. *Most shops open in the afternoons and close around 2300. Map 5, E7, p254* Tiny stalls selling unusual clothes, shoes and accessories.

Chater House, Chater Rd, Central. *Map 2, E9, p249* For serious shoppers seeking the likes of Armani, Prada and Bvlgari, with tasteful florists and cosmetics stores. Links by walkway to Prince's Building, with a similar range.

Festival Walk, Tat Chee Av, Kowloon Tong. *1030-2000.* Huge, with a great feeling of space, yet relatively uncrowded. Has good selection of mid-range stores like Esprit, Mango and Wrangler, plus an ice-skating rink, cinemas and great restaurants.

The Landmark, 16 Des Voeux Rd, Central. *Map 2, F8, p249* An elegant mall set around a huge central atrium, with designers like Versace, Dior, and Armani. Links up with Prince's Building.

Lane Crawford, 70 Queen's Rd, Central, **T** 2118 3388. *1000-1900, Mon-Sat. Map 2, E7, p249* 1-3 The Mall, Pacific Pl, 88 Queensway, Admiralty, **T** 2845 1838. *1000-2100. Map 3, F2, p250* Hong Kong's oldest western-style department store, catering to the city's wealthiest and most chic with top designer labels and only the best in household wares.

Pacific Place, 88 Queensway, Admiralty. *Map 3, F2, p250* Spacious, spread over four floors, its stores range from casual wear, fashion boutiques to top designers. Also has cinemas and restaurants.

Seibu, 88 Queensway Pacific Pl, **T** 2877 3627, 2868 0111. *1030-2000 Sun-Wed, 1030-2100 Thu-Sat. Map 3, F2, p250* Windsor House, 311 Gloucester Rd, Causeway Bay, **T** 2890 0333. *Map 4, D7, p253* One of Japan's largest department stores housing an upmarket collection of chic designers, mainly European, houseware and gifts, and a great food department with imported items unavailable elsewhere.

Sogo, 555 Hennessy Rd, Causeway Bay, **T** 2833 8338. *1100-2300. Map 4, D5, p252* Huge Japanese department store with designer clothes, accessories, electrical and household goods, shoes, cosmetics, and a popular Japanese supermarket. Information and money exchange counter on the ground floor.

Times Square, 2 Matheson St, Causeway Bay. *Map 4, F3, p252* Set over nine floors, this is a popular meeting place and has a wide variety of outlets, including a great food court in the basement. Dazzling decorations outside especially during major festivals.

Discount designer stores

Unofficial stores with racks of cheap designer goods are dotted around Wan Chai, Causeway Bay, and Granville Rd in Tsim Sha Tsui.

Joyce Warehouse, 21/F Horizon Plaza, 2 Lee Wing St, Ap Lei Chau, **T** 2814 8313. Huge discounts on designer names like Galliano, Issey Miyake and D&G, usually on items over a year old.

Labels For Less, 3008-3011 International Finance Centre, Harbour View Rd, Central, **T** 2295 3881. *Map 2, C9, p249* Discounts on Givenchy, Christian Lacroix and Roberto Cavali.

I.T. Sale Shop, 72-119, 3/F Silvercord, Tsim Sha Tsui, **T** 2377 9466. *Map 5, I3, p255* Up to 80% discounts on less widespread labels such as Alexander McQueen, Camper and Christophe Lemaire.

Pedder Building,12 Pedder St, Central. *Most stores 1000-1900. Map 2, F9, p249* Eight floors of small clothes shops, many of which carry good discount on designer names.

Sample King, 16 Johnston Rd, Wan Chai. *Map 3, G6, p250* Casual clothing by Ralph Lauren, Nicole Farhi and Guess.

Super Sample, 35-45 Johnston Rd, Wan Chai. *Map 3, G6, p250* Try your luck and scour the racks and you may find Cacharel evening wear or Calvin Klein undies for next to nothing.

Dried seafood

The best area for dried seafood and exotic 'tonic' goods is around **Des Voeux Road West** and **Bonham Strand West** (see p37) where the specialist shops have dried scallop, ginseng and bird's nest by the bucketful.

Electronic and computers

Fortress Shop, No. 70, 2/F Tower II, Admiralty Centre, **T** 2866 2461. *1000-1900. Map 3, G2, p250* 3/F Capitol Centre, Jardine Bazaar, Causeway Bay, **T** 3162 8750. *1100-2200. Map 4, E6, p252* G/F Yu Sung Boon Bldg, 107 Des Voeux Rd, Central, **T** 2544 4385. *1030-1930. Map 2, C7, p249* B/F Melbourne Plaza, 33 Queen's Rd, Central, **T** 2121 1077. *1000-2000. Map 2, F7, p249* G/F Hopewell Centre, 183 Queen's Rd East, Wan Chai, **T** 2866 3138. *1100-2100. Map 3, H7, p251* G/F Hong Kong Plaza, 188 Connaught Rd West, Sheung Wan, **T** 2549 8320. *1100- 2100. Map 2, A2, p248* **Fortress World** Shops 1-6, Basements 1 & 2, Chuang's London Plaza, 219 Nathan Rd, Jordan, **T** 2736 8485. *1100-2100. Map 5, D4, p254* A large chain with countless more stores throughout the territory, and a reliable store with decent prices and service, selling most things electrical.

Golden Shopping Arcade, 156 Fuk Wah St, Sham Shui Po, Kowloon. Known for its cheap deals and pirate software, although best if you know exactly what you're looking for.

Windsor House, 311 Gloucester Rd, Causeway Bay. *Map 4, D7, p253* A shopping mall specializing in hardware and software, and shopping around is essential to get an idea of prices. Check carefully for the guarantees on new equipment.

Fashion

As well as designer labels, there are plenty of good-value local stores selling casual gear, especially in the many outlets of Bossini, Giordano, U2 and 2000. See also Department stores above.

Blanc De Chine, 201-203 Pedder Bldg, 12 Pedder St, Central, **T** 2524 7875. *1000-1900 Mon-Sat. 1200-1700 Sun and public holidays. Map 2, F8, p249* Small store with exquisite (and prices to match) designer clothes which combine traditional Chinese styles with a contemporary twist. Even supplies the great Jackie Chan.

Shanghai Tang Pedder Building, Pedder St, Central, **T** 2525 7333. *Map 2, F8, p249* The Peninsula Hotel, Shop ML1-3, Tsim Sha Tsui, **T** 2537 2888. *Map 5, K4, p255* Owned by millionaire local entrepreneur David Tang and chock-full of funky Chinese-influenced clothes. Renowned for its trademark luminous green- and pink-padded jackets, plus household furnishings and trinkets.

Vivienne Tam Shop, 209 Pacific Pl, 88 Queensway, Central, **T** 2523 6620. *Map 3, F2, p250* This Hong Kong-born New York-based designer has combined her Chinese roots with funky prints Warhol style, and is famous for her silk jackets and t-shirts emblazoned with Mao images.

Walter Ma, B1-B2, 1-13 Century Sq, D'Aguilar St, Central, **T** 2840 1266. *Map 2, F7, p249* 49A Kimberly Rd, Tsim Sha Tsui, **T** 2739 4022. *Map 5, F5, p254* One of the best local designers, creating zany fashions for the smart, young party crowd. Vee is his less costly line.

Jewellery and watches

Most of the top jewellers are in the upmarket malls, but more mainstream stores are dotted around the shopping areas. Jade fans should visit the **Jade Market**, Kansu St, Jordan, *1000-1600*, for trinkets and jewellery at a wide range prices. Freshwater pearls are widely available in **Stanley Market**. Cheap, plastic watches in fun designs are all over **Temple Street** and **Stanley Market**.

3D-Gold, 28 Man Lok St, Hunghom, Kowloon, **T** 2766 3332. *0900-1800*. Jewellery showroom with exotic exhibits; a must for fans of all things gold.

Chow Tai Fook Jewellery, G/F Causeway Bay Plaza, Phase 1, 489 Hennessy Rd, Causeway Bay, **T** 2838 6222. *1030-2200*. *Map 4, D4, p252* Renowned for its good service and decent prices.

Just Gold Shop, 512 Times Square, Causeway Bay, **T** 2895 7128. *Map 4, F3, p252* A2 27 Nathan Rd, Tsim Sha Tsui. **T** 2312 1120. *0800-2000*. *Map 5, J4, p255* Mid-priced chain with many outlets, specializing in yellow gold in fashionable designs.

! Hong Kong loves its superlatives, but the world's most expensive gold toilet and washroom, as included in the Guinness Book of Records, must be the most original. Built by 3D-Gold and worth HK$38m, it is made of 380kg of gold and 6200 pieces of precious stones and pearls, and can be viewed (but not used) at their Kowloon showroom.

Opal Mine Shop, G & H, G/F Burlington Arcade, 92 Nathan Rd, Tsim Sha Tsui, **T** 2721 9933. *0930-1900*. *Map 5, G4, p255* A simulated opal mining cave, which mines, cuts and sells black, crystal and white opals, mounted onto gold.

Markets

Jardine's Crescent, Causeway Bay, and **The Lanes**, Central, both have low-cost clothes, watches, jewellery and knick-knacks crammed into narrow streets. Both get crowded especially in the evenings but make for some entertaining browsings.

Bird Market, Yuen Po Street Bird Garden, Mongkok. *0700-1900*. *Map 6, p256 See also p76* Traditional Chinese garden which is the meeting place for all those buying and selling birds, cages and food.

Cat Street, off Hollywood Rd, Central. *Map 2, C2, p248 See also p48* Flea market with a few stalls with junk or antiques, depending on your luck at browsing, like ornamental birdcages, jade bracelets and replica snuff bottles, plus second-hand stuff.

Flower Market, Flower Market Street, Mongkok. *Map 6, p256 See p76* Entire street devoted to wholesale and retail flower shops, busiest during Chinese New Year.

Ladies Market, Tung Choi St, Mongkok. *Map 6, p256 See also p78* Stalls piled with clothes, cheap but hardly stylish, household goods, with the Goldfish Market at the southern end of the street.

Stanley Market, Stanley. *Map 1, G6, p247 See also p65* An excellent day out, as well as a great selection of silk ties, Chinese clothes, knock-off designer labels, shoes, accessories, freshwater pearls, toys and handicrafts.

Temple Street Night Market, Temple St, Jordan. *Map 5, A3, p254 See also p75* Highly recommended for its entertainment value if not for its goods. Comes alive in the evenings and sells clothes, souvenirs, cheap watches, CDs, and anything else you can stuff in your suitcase.

Music

HMV, 5/F Sands Bldg, 17 Hankow Rd, Tsim Sha Tsui, **T** 2302 0122. *0900-2345*. *Map 5, I4, p255* Spread over four floors, this is Hong Kong's largest music store with UK chart and dance, classical, Cantopop, jazz, DVDs and videos. Sales bring the prices crashing down. Also branches at Central Building, Pedder St, Central and Windsor House, Causeway Bay, **T** 2504 3669.

Tom Lee Music, G/F, 1-9 Cameron Lane, Tsim Sha Tsui, **T** 2723 9932. *1000-2100*. *Map 5, G5, p255* 144-149 Gloucester Rd, Wan Chai, **T** 2519 0238. *1000-2000*. *Map 3, D11, p251* A long-standing music outlet with many more stores around the city, Tom Lee has a huge range of musical instruments, from keyboards and violins to specialist Asian instruments.

Photographic equipment

Stanley Street, Central (see p45), is the best place for reputable camera shops, some of which have second-hand gear and also sell and process colour and black and white films. Although not necessarily the cheapest, these are among the most reliable.

Fortress Zoom, G/F, Mohan Building, 14 Hankow Rd, Tsim Sha Tsui, **T** 2311 2318. *1000-2100*. *Map 5, I4, p255* G/F 59 Russell St, Causeway Bay, **T** 2504 4525. *1100-2300*. *Map 4, E4, p252* Part of the huge Fortress chain of electronic shops, these give a good indication of prices, which are fixed and low.

Photo Scientific, 6 Stanley St, Central, **T** 2525 0550. *1000-1900. Map 2, F7, p249* Friendly and knowledgeable staff and a good place to start for prices and information, selling digital and video cameras and accessories, and some second-hand gear.

Tailors

There are countless bespoke tailors advertised widely, but check how long each one will take if your stay is a short one. As always, look for the Quality Tourism Services sign.

Sam's Tailor, Burlington Arcade, 92-94 Nathan Rd, Tsim Sha Tsui, **T** 2367 9423, www.samstailor.com *Map 5, G4, p255* Hong Kong's best-known tailor, having sewn the suits of stars for decades, and definitely worth the hype. Now with a large staff, they make men's and women's suits from scratch, or copy your favourite item, quickly.

Toys

Toys 'R' Us, B/F Shop 032, Ocean Terminal, Tsim Sha Tsui, **T** 2730 9462. *Map 5, K1, p255* Said to be the world's largest toy store. 1/F Windsor House, 311 Gloucester Rd, Causeway Bay, **T** 2881 1728. *1000-2200. MTR: Causeway Bay. Map 4, D7, p253*

Toys Club Unit, 901 9/F Horizon Plaza, 2 Lee Wing St, Ap Lei Chau, **T** 2836 0875. *1100-1900.* Warehouse prices for toys, clothes and books.

Hong Kong is not renowned for its sporting culture, perhaps because of its confined spaces and often unsuitable climate. Most locals have, at some time, dabbled in Tai Chi but you will rarely see kids kick a **football** around, mainly because of lack of space and because public parks are not really seen as makeshift pitches. That said, China's qualification for the 2002 World Cup brought great enthusiasm and thousands watched their games on huge open-air TV screens. Hong Kong has always been pretty keen on racket sports like **badminton**, **squash** and **table tennis**, and there has been an increased interest in **surfing** and other **watersports**, probably inspired by their very heroine Lee Lai-shan who in 1996 won their first ever Olympic gold medal. You can participate in a good selection of watersports, from water-skiing lessons and renting bodyboards to diving, although the warm, safe waters of Hong Kong may not be everyone's idea of adventure. The biggest and noisiest sporting event is the annual **Rugby 7s**, attracting visitors from all over the world and turning the city into an unofficial beer fest when the day's play has ended and partying continues till dawn.

Cricket

Domestic cricket consists of the Saturday League (17 teams, recreational) and Sunday League (8 teams, serious) and from these players the Hong Kong team is selected. The national team has enjoyed some success in recent years, with ambitions to qualify for the World Cup. You can watch local games at the **Hong Kong Cricket Club**, Magazine Gap Rd, **T** 2574 6266, and the **Kowloon Cricket Club**, 10 Cox's Rd, Jordan, **T** 2367 4141. Details of fixtures are in the *South China Morning Post* and *The Standard*. **Hong Kong Cricket Association**, **T** 2504 8101, www.hkca.cricket.org

   Hong Kong Cricket 6s, Kowloon Cricket Club. Hong Kong's biggest annual cricket tournament is the explosive 6-a-side game that seems to suit the atmosphere of the city. With most of the international test-playing teams plus Hong Kong, the competition in early November attracts expats and visitors.

Fitness

South China Athletic Stadium, 88 Caroline Hill Rd, Causeway Bay, **T** 2577 6932. *Map 4, G7/8, p253* No-frills gym, run by the council.

Salisbury YMCA, 41 Salisbury Rd, Tsim Sha Tsui, **T** 2369 2211. *Map 5, J3, p255*

New York Fitness, 1-2/F Kinwick Centre, 32 Hollywood Rd, Central, **T** 2543 2280. *Map 2, F5, p248*

Football

Although hugely popular during the 70s and 80s, domestic football has suffered a slump mainly because many good overseas players had to be sold, and the European matches are now broadcast regularly on Star TV – the English Premier League being especially popular. The best two teams in the league are South China and Happy Valley, and two decent grounds are **Hong Kong Football Club Stadium** 3 Sports Rd, Happy Valley (adjacent to the racecourse), **T** 2576 8576, *Map 4, H3, p252*, and **Mongkok**, 37 Flower Market Rd, Mongkok, **T** 2380 0188. Check the sports pages for fixtures.

The biggest and most popular tournament is the **Carlsberg Cup**, played on the first three days of Chinese New Year at the National Stadium. Three national teams plus Hong Kong play a round-robin tournament, although the home side never pull any real surprises as they have problems in qualifying to get anywhere in the Asia Cup, let alone the World Cup.

Golf

Golf is hugely popular but expensive. Non-members can usually use private clubs during weekdays, sometimes daytime only. Hong Kong is the venue for prestigious international tournaments like the Omega Hong Kong Open (late Nov/early Dec).

Hong Kong Golf Association, **T** 2522 8804, www.hkga.com, has information on tournaments as well as driving ranges. Because of the high prices of playing, many locals hop over the border into China, which offers great golfing at a fraction of the price, especially at **Missions Hill** in Shenzen, where Tiger Woods has played.

Clearwater Bay Golf and Country Club, 139 Tai Au Mun Rd, Clearwater Bay, **T** 2719 1595, www.cwbgolf.org *0900-2400 Mon-Fri.* $1400/18 holes, club hire $300.

Kau Sai Chau Public Golf Course, Kau Sai Chau Island, off Sai Kung, **T** 2791 3388, www.kscgolf.com *0700-2200, 0700-2000 Mon and Thu.* Prices vary according to course, time and day. $330-500/9

All's fair in love and penalties

The 2003 Carlsberg Cup was best remembered for a single sporting gesture: in the game between Iran and Denmark, a mischievous spectator blew a whistle and Iran's Alireza Vahedinikbakt picked up the ball, thinking it was half-time. The ref awarded Denmark a penalty for hand-ball, and the furious Iranian team were about to walk out. The Danish coach indicated they would forfeit the penalty, so when Morten Olsen stepped up for the spot kick, he deliberately kicked the ball towards the corner flag, a great sporting act for which he was nominated for a FIFA Fair Play Award by the Iranian manager.

holes. $550-900/18 holes, club hire $150. Hong Kong's only public golf club has four courses, one of which is championship, so the standard and facilities here are excellent.

Obstacle Golf Course, Shek O Beach. *0800-1700 Dec-Feb, 0900-1800 Mar-Nov*. $13/game/person. Hardly championship calibre but a bit of fun, right next to the beach.

Macau Golf and Country Club, Estrada de Hac Sa, Coloane, Macau, **T** 871 188, www.macaugolfandcountryclub.com *0630-1900 Mon-Fri*. 9 holes $500, 18 holes $700. Club hire extra. The only golf course in Macau, this rather exclusive club is open to non-members provided they are staying in certain hotels.

Hiking

As over 70% of Hong Kong is too steep to be developed, the rocky coasts, woodlands and hills on the outlying islands and New Territories are perfect for hiking, which provides a great way of discovering the wilder side of life. The government has always developed and maintained trails and country parks, the most famous of which is the **MacLehose Trail** (see p88), and there are good guides and maps available of treks and walks of all lengths and standards. Two of the best are *Exploring Hong Kong's Countryside - A Visitor's Companion* (Edward Stokes) and *South China Morning Post Hiking Guide* which has great pull-out maps. The best time for hiking is between the cooler months of September and April. See also p103.

Horse racing

Hong Kong See p54 and 90.

Ice-skating

Festival Walk Glacier, Festival Walk, Kowloon Tong, **T** 2844 3588. *1030-2200 Mon-Fri, 0830-2200 Sat, 1300-1730 Sun.* $60. A great rink in this attractive and relatively uncrowded shopping centre. Very busy during weekends and school holidays.

Kayaking

Guided hiking tours with kayaking around remote parts of Sai Kung are organized by Paul Etherington, affiliated to the Hong Kong Tourist Board, **T** 9300 5197, www.kayak-and-hike.com $450 per person. Kayaking around bays and coral reefs.

Mountain biking

Hong Kong Moutain Bike Association, www.hkmba.org Web-based organization successfully promoting multi-use trails, seven of which are listed on its website including Dragon's Back (near Shek O) and Chi Ma Wan, and Discovery Bay to Nim Shue Wan. Bikes can be rented from around $50/day on Lantau and other biking areas.

Sports

Paragliding

Hong Kong Paragliding Association, T 2559 7347, 9778 2116. Although there are no places for learning, those with a paragliding license, recognized by the Hong Kong Paragliding Association, may take advantage of great gliding above Shek O, Sai Wan and Lantau.

Rugby

Hong Kong Rugby Sevens, Hong Kong Rugby Football Union, Rm 2001, Sports House, 1 Stadium Path, So Kon Po, Causeway Bay, **T** 2504 8311, www.hksevens.com.hk See p180. This huge event every April sees around 24 teams from around the world, from Australia to Russia, participate.

Squash, badminton and table tennis

Kowloon Park Sports Centre, 22 Austin Rd, Tsim Sha Tsui, **T** 2724 3120, 2724 3344. Squash ($27/30mins) badminton ($59/hour) and table tennis ($21/hour) are all available at the modern centre, and booking is advised especially evenings and weekends. Bring passport or other ID.

Harbour Rd Indoor Games Hall, 27 Harbour Rd, Wan Chai, **T** 2827 9684.

Swimming

Kowloon Park, Tsim Sha Tsui, **T** 2724 4522, 2724 3577. *0630-1200, 1300-1700 and 1800-2200.* Adults $19, concs $9. The best place by far with three outdoor (Apr-Oct) and two indoor pools (Jun-Mar) in the middle of the park, which includes an Olympic-sized pool often the venue of galas. Great for children.

Tennis

Hong Kong Tennis Centre, Wong Nai Chung Gap Rd, Happy Valley, **T** 2574 9122.

Victoria Park, Hing Fat St, Causeway Bay, **T** 2570 6186.

Watersports

Watersports have enjoyed a revival and there are many beaches around Hong Kong revered in the international surfing scene, even though the water isn't always that clean or exciting. Diving is possible, although there is far better diving elsewhere in Asia. **Big Wave Bay**, near Shek O, is surfers' paradise and **Tai Long Wan** in Sai Kung has bigger waves, although is less accessible.

Xtreme Wake Boarding, 16 Repulse Bay, Beach Rd, **T** 2592 7238, project-XTREME@hongkong.com English-speaking instructor, **T** 6076 7524. Shop on the beach hires equipment.

Chong Hing Water Sports Centre, Sai Kung, **T** 2792 6810. Sampans and pedal-boats for hire for those with watersport proficiency certificates.

Jockey Club Wong Shek Water Sports Centre, Sai Kung, **T** 2328 2311, and **Tai Mei Tuk Water Sports Centre**, Tai Po, **T** 2665 3591, both hire canoes, dinghies and windsurfs for those with certificates. Training courses also offered.

Cheung Chau Windsurfing Centre, Hai Pak Rd, Tung Wan Beach, Cheung Chau, **T** 2981 8316. Where Lee Lai Shan (see p104) learnt her trade. A popular and attractive beach.

Hong Kong's gay scene is relatively open, considering that male homosexuality was decriminalized as recently as 1991 and now is permitted between two consenting males over 21, in private. (There are no laws concerning sex between women.) Since then, the local gay and lesbian community, known as *tongzhi*, has become more socially acceptable, and there's a vibrant gay scene especially around Central and SoHo. Attitudes towards gay and lesbian people within Chinese society are hesitant, with the usual difficulties of coming out to family and colleagues, but it is becoming easier mainly because Hong Kong is one of the most liberal cities in Asia. Gay couples will occasionally walk hand-in-hand around Central or Wan Chai, if not around housing estates or villages in the outskirts. The late 1990s saw a new wave of gay saunas, bars and bookshops, and there are nearly 20 organizations holding events and conferences, including the **Rainbow Festival**, **Lesbian and Gay Film Festival**, and the **International Tongzhi Conference**. The biggest cloud hanging over the gay community since 1997 is the implications of Article 23 and its subversion laws (see p15).

Beaches

Cheung Sha, Lantau. *Map 6, p256* The middle area of the beach is a popular gay hang-out with a couple of decent restaurants close by, changing rooms and shower, and a shop to rent beach umbrellas and mats.

Middle Bay, South Bay Rd. *Map 1, F5, p247* A short walk from Repulse Bay, this is the best gay beach and a good cruising spot.

Bars and clubs

HH = Happy Hour.

Club 64, 12-14 Wing Wah Lane, Central, **T** 2523 2801. *1430-0200 Mon-Thu, 1430-0300 Fri-Sat, 1800-0100 Sun. HH 1430-2100.* *Map 2, F6, p248 See also p158* A gay-friendly, liberal atmosphere with cheap drinks and a mixed crowd of students, artists and musicians, always busy at weekends.

Club 97, 9 Lan Kwai Fong, Central, **T** 2810 9333. *1800-0200 Mon-Thu, 1800-0400 Fri-Sun, HH 1800-2200 Mon-Thu.* *Map 2, G6, p248 See also p159* Like its sister venue Post 97, Club has been a long-standing favourite haunt with the gay crowd, ever since the old days of the masked, underpants-clad Man in the Cage (sadly no more). Gay happy hour (*1800-2200 Fri*) is one of the most popular nights in the area, and a great start to the weekend.

Home, 2/F23 Hollywood Rd, Central, **T** 2545 0023. *2100-late Mon-Thu, 2100-0900 Fri-Sat.* *Map 2, F5, p248 See also p160* Not exclusively gay, but a mixed club which is still open long after everything else has shut. Often open till 1100, it is regarded as a recovery room for war-torn party queens and even serves breakfast with English tea.

Gay and lesbian

▶ Pink finance

Hong Kong has been encouraged to tap into the "pink dollar" and become Asia's leading gay tourist destination, although the Tourist Board has no official policy yet on attracting gay visitors. Legislators have been touted with the idea of hosting a street carnival for the world's gay and lesbian community, inspired by the success of Sydney's world-famous Mardi Gras. Hong Kong, naturally, is more inspired by the potential financial benefits of the high-spending, child-free, disposable-income-laden gay tourist, than the willingness to eliminate sexual taboos and discrimination, but at least it's an excuse to party.

Liquid, 1-5 Elgin St, Central, **T** 2549 8386. *1800-late Tue-Fri, 2000-late Sat-Sun. Map 2, E4, p248 See also p160* A large good-vibe venue, the gay happy hour (*1800-2200 Fri*) is a popular addition to this trendy club.

New Wally Matt Lounge, G/F 5A Humphrey's Av, Tsim Sha Tsui, **T** 2721 2568, enquiry@wallymatt.com *1700-0400. HH 1700-2200. Map 5, H5, p255* Like the Bar and Lounge (see below), it has been refurbished and reopened, and is more like the original Wally Matts. Good, friendly place for a relaxed drink before moving on. Billed as the first internet gay bar in Hong Kong.

one-fifth, 1/F Starcrest, 9 Star St, Wan Chai, **T** 2520 2515. Corner of Wing Fung St. *1800-0100 Mon-Wed, 1800-0200 Thu, 1800-0300 Fri, 2000-0300 Sat, HH 1800-2100. Map 3, G4, p250 See also p161* Not billed as a gay bar, but popular with the smart lesbian scene.

Post 97, UG/F 9 Lan Kwai Fong, Central, **T** 2186 1837. *HH 1700-1900 (Mon-Fri). Map 2, G6/7, p248 See also p139* Gay-friendly

Gay and lesbian

café/bar/restaurant with a chilled-out atmosphere during the afternoon, and a positively pumping one late-night at weekends.

Propaganda, LG/F 1 Hollywood Rd, Central, **T** 2868 1316. *2100-0330 Mon-Thu, 2100-0500 Fri-Sat. Map 2, F6, p248* One of the first gay clubs in Hong Kong, Propaganda enjoys its new venue and is still the most popular and packed, attracting celebs and the in-crowd, playing house and funk.

Rice Bar, G/F 33 Jervois St, Sheung Wan, **T** 2851 4800. *1830-0100 Sun-Thu, 1830-0200 Fri, 2000-0300 Sat. HH 1830-2100. Map 2, C3, p248 See also p160* A comfortable, relaxed bar to start or end the evening with DJs most night, and a mixed crowd.

Tony's Bar, G/F 7-9 Bristol Av, Tsim Sha Tsui, **T** 2723 2726. *Map 5, I5, p255* Friendly staff and a very mixed, down-to-earth crowd, less showy and dressy than many gay bars on Hong Kong Island.

Tower Club, 20-22 D'Aguilar St, Central, **T** 2525 6118. *HH 1800-2100. Map 2, G6/7, p248* One of the earliest gay joints in Lan Kwai Fong, this is a huge bar known for its cocktails and shooters, with smaller rooms for 6-8 people and a terrace.

Wally Matt Bar and Lounge, G/F 3 Granville Circuit, Tsim Sha Tsui, **T** 2367 6874, wm@wallymatt.com.hk *1700-0400. Behind the Ramada Hotel on Chatham Road. Map 5, G6, p255* This is one of the oldest gay bars in Hong Kong, the first of two Wally Matts and has been recently revamped with a more techno look. A relaxed, mixed crowd.

Works, 1/F 30-32 Wyndham St, Central, **T** 2868 6102. *1900-0200. HH 1900-2100. Map 2, G6, p248* A sister club of Propaganda in its original venue. This is not as refined or trendy but a rougher, sleazier atmosphere and a good pick-up joint.

Zip, G/F 2 Glenealy, Central, **T** 2523 3595. *1800-0200.* *Map 2, H5, p248* Very trendy with an outdoor covered patio.

Bookshops

There no specifically gay bookshops, but larger stores will have a small section of gay and lesbian literature. (See p191, bookshops).

Events

Tongzhi Conference, tongzhiconference@yahoo.com An international conference for Chinese lesbians, gays, bisexuals and transexuals. Held around October every two years, 2003, 2005 etc.

Organizations

Chi Heng Foundation, Box 3923, GPO, Central, **T** 2517 0564, www.chihengfoundation.com Lesbian and Gay organization with advice, and actively working for *tongzhi* equality.

Tongzhi Archive, tongzhiarchive@yahoo.com An archive and research centre for tongzhi history and the community.

Aids Hotline, **T** 2780 2211, www.27802211.com

Dr Sex Hotline, **T** 2337 2121, www.dsonline.com.hk A free sexual health advice line.

Saunas

Rainbow, 46/52 Temple St, Yau Ma Tei, **T** 2385 6652. *1300-2400.* *Map 5, A3, p254* A good, mixed, friendly crowd, English spoken.

Hong Kong is a positive delight for children, and the tourist brochure cliché "something for everyone" is, for once, spot on. A temple with incense and worshippers burning paper money, the novelty of night markets or even seeing live frogs or snakes for sale will provoke wide-eyed amazement in kids of all ages. There are plenty of child-friendly theme parks, playgrounds and museums with wonderful interactive displays. Add the view of the night skyline, travelling on boats, country parks, theme parks and of course beaches and even the most demanding of children will be enthralled. Chinese families often bring their children for late-night shopping, eating and entertainment; none of that curfew culture here. In fact, having a baby or small child will bring you instant friends, bridging both cultural and language barriers. The streets and public transport at night are safer than most cities in the world; the main problem will be getting around congested streets with a pushchair – people tend to carry their kids in their arms or a sling. And, if little Jonny or Jane can't bear the thought of fried squid or spicy tofu, there are plenty of western restaurants and cafés to feed them.

★ Kids' stuff

- **Restaurant** *Marché* p145. Paper plates on tiny tables for the kids, good choice of food and cocktails for adults, and the best harbour views.
- **Hotel** *YMCA The Salisbury* p123 (urban) for good activities, or *Silvermine Beach Hotel* p127 (rural) for the peaceful location on Miu Wo beach.
- **Museum** *Museum of History* p74 for the huge and stunning Hong Kong Story (older), and Science Museum p74 for hands-on colourful activities (younger).
- **Day out** *The Peak* p60 for walks, views, entertainment and food.
- **Market** *Stanley* (p65) Easy to wander around and plenty of waterside restaurants.

Sights and activities

Dolphinwatch. Pick up at Mandarin Oriental east lobby, *0830*, and Kowloon Hotel, *0900*. **T** 2984 1414, www.hkdolphinwatch.com *$320, $160 children under 12*. 3-5 days weekly, depending on season. Phone to check and book. The half-day boat trip sails to the Pearl River Delta, home to 1000 pink Indo-pacific humpback dolphins.

Duk Ling ride, from Kowloon public pier, Tsim Sha Tsui, or Queen's Pier, Central. Register at **T** 2508 1234. *Deps at 1400, 1500, 1600 and 1700 Thu. Free. See also p32* The one-hour sail on a restored traditional Chinese junk is a great way of reliving history and touring around the harbour. May be a little choppy for young kids. A more interesting alternative to the Star Ferry.

Cheung Chau *See also p104* This outlying island has the advantage of having no cars, so getting around is done by either hiring bikes or being pedalled around on a two-seater pedicab. Try to spot a tiny fire engine or ambulance, the only vehicles on the road. A walk around the waterfront to the Cheung Po Tsai cave, said to be the HQ of a local pirate, or a scramble along the rocks is good fun for older kids. There is a marked Family Trail from Cheung Kwai Road to a reservoir with great views.

Festivals. *See p177.* Check which festivals coincide with your visit as many attractions and celebrations appeal to kids, especially the Dragon Boat Festival, Chinese New Year, Spring Lantern Festival, Cheung Chau Bun Festival and the Mid-Autumn Festival.

Festival Walk Glacier, Festival Walk, 80 Tat Chee Ave, Kowloon Tong, **T** 2844 3588. *1030-2200 Mon-Thu, 0830-2200 Sat, 1300-1730 Sun. $60. See also p206* The city's largest ice-skating rink in one of the most spacious and least crowded shopping malls in Hong Kong.

Hong Kong Science Museum, 2 Science Museum Rd, Tsim Sha Tsui E, **T** 2732 3232. *See also p74* The Children's Discovery Gallery, is a wonderful interactive collection of exhibits and activities, where kids can sit inside models of village houses watching videos of village life. There is a reconstruction of Mai Po Marshes, and other activities for younger visitors.

Hong Kong tram. *0600-2400. $2, $1 children. See also p30* Hopping on the top deck of a tram from Kennedy Town to Causeway Bay to gaze at the crowds below saves the legs but not the senses, but hold on to little ones near open windows.

Kowloon Park, 22 Austin Rd, Tsim Sha Tsui. *See also p72* Away from the shops and crowds, the welcome green space has the addition of Kung Fu Corner, *Sun 1430-1630*, with free demonstrations and activities, plus the Sculpture Park, outdoor swimming pools, children's playground and bird lake.

Lamma Island *See also p103* A trip out on a ferry to Lamma and some good walking, beaches and waterfront dining. A relatively easy walk for children is between Yung Shue Wan and Sok Kwu Wan, about an hour along a well-marked path.

Mid-levels escalator to Hollywood Road. Travelling uphill between 1020-2400. *See also p46* Another great way to gaze at leisure at the sights and sounds above and below, and kids will be amazed at the world's longest escalator.

Mongkok. *See also p75* If walking through crowded markets is a problem, the charming Yuen Po Street Bird Garden is set in Chinese-style gardens where people come to buy and sell tiny songbirds and parrots in ornate wooden cages.

Obstacle Golf Course, Shek O Beach. *0800-1700 Dec-Feb, 0900-1800 Mar-Nov*. Each game $13/person. A small crazy golf course on the beach.

Ocean Park, Aberdeen, **T** 2552 0291, www.oceanpark.com.hk *1000-1800. $180, $90 children*. One of the largest oceanarium and theme parks in Southeast Asia, with educational and entertainment features. Their research centre led to the birth of two dolphins in 2001, there are 70 sharks in the Shark Aquarium, and two pandas inside the Giant Panda Habitat. The two sections are connected by a 200 m cable-car with fantastic views. Also a Butterfly House, Dinosaur Discover Trail, Amazing Amazon Whisker's Wild Ride and Kid's World area for younger visitors.

The Peak: The Peak Tower, 128 Peak Rd. *0700-2400*. **Peak Galleria** 118 Peak Rd, **T** 2849 4113. *1000-2200*. *See also p60* With walks, food, views and shops, the Peak can easily make a whole day out. The Peak Tower has good child-friendly restaurants (and ice cream parlours), a viewing platform and a small kids' playground. Peak Galleria opposite has an easy-going shopping mall with some kitsch souvenirs. **Peak Explorer Motion Simulator**, Level 4, The Peak Tower. *1200-2140 Mon-Fri, 0930-2140 Sat-Sun and public holidays. $52, $35 children.* Strap the kids in and let them (nearly) experience a wild ride into space. Recommended. **Madame Tussaud's**, Level 2 The Peak Tower, **T** 2849 2788. *1100-2000 Sun-Thu, 1100-2100 Fri-Sat. $75, $50 children.* Asia's first, where David Beckham meets Jackie Chan. **Ripley's Believe It or Not Odditorium**, Level 3, The Peak Tower, **T** 2849 0668. *0930-2200. $75, $50 children.* Eleven themed galleries with hundreds of bizarre facts from around the world.

Snoopy's World Level 3 Podium, New Town Plaza, Sha Tin, **T** 2601 9178. *1000-2000.* The world's second outdoor Peanuts playground brings together more than 60 Peanuts figures, including a giant Snoopy on his kennel, in six amusement zones. Free body painting and balloons.

Stanley Market, Stanley. *1000-1700. See also p65* Of all the markets in Hong Kong, Stanley has the advantage of also being near a beach. There is a laid-back, holiday feel to the place, and the bright and cheerful stalls are chock-full of souvenirs, clothes and toys. The bus ride from Central is spectacular.

Teddy Bear Kingdom, The Amazon, 12 Salisbury Rd, Tsim Sha Tsui, **T** 2130 2130, www.teddybearkingdom.com.hk *1000-2200.* Housed inside the Amazon mall, it contains the Teddy Bear Museum with 400 bears, including one made from gold. Kids can make their own bears and the Carnival Forest has 100 games. There are performances and entertainment every afternoon at the Picnic Palace. *Adults $50, children (3-11) $50.*

Airline offices

Aeroflot, **T** 2845 4232. **Air Canada**, **T** 2867 8111. **Air France**, **T** 2524 8145. **Aer Lingus**, **T** 2822 9090. **Air New Zealand**, **T** 2524 9041. **American Airlines**, **T** 2826 9102. **British Airways**, **T** 2822 9090. **Continental Airlines**, **T** 3198 5577. **Gulf Air**, **T** 2882 2892. **Hong Kong Dragonair**, **T** 3193 3888. **KLM**, **T** 2808 2111. **Lufthansa**, **T** 2868 2313. **Malaysian Airlines**, **T** 2521 8181. **Philippines Airlines**, **T** 2301 9300. **Qantas**, **T** 2822 9000. **Singapore Airlines**, **T** 2520 2233. **US Airways**, **T** 3110 3668. **United Airlines**, **T** 2810 4888. **Virgin Atlantic**, **T** 2532 6060.

Banks and ATMs

Banks and ATMs are everywhere and will take most overseas debit and credit cards. Banking hours are usually *0900-1630 Mon-Fri, 0900-1200 Sat*. In Macau you are able to withdraw either Hong Kong dollars or patacas, which are worth around the same. Dollars can be used in Macau, but patacas aren't accepted in Hong Kong.

Bicycle hire

Forget cycling in the city; there are places for hiring bikes on arrival at Mui Wo, Cheung Chau, Lamma and Shek O. Around $30-40/day.

Car hire

Rented cars are so rarely needed in Hong Kong as public transport and taxis are so widespread and good value. Chauffeur-driven cars are available from most top hotels.

Consulates and embassies

Australia, 24/F Harbour Centre, 25 Harbour Rd, Wan Chai, **T** 2827 8881. **Canada**, 11/F-14/F One Exchange Sq, 8 Connaught Pl, Central, **T** 2810 4321. **France**, 26/F Admiralty Centre Tower 2, 18 Harcourt Rd, **T** 3196 6100. **New Zealand**, 3414 Jardine House, Connaught Rd, Central, **T** 2525 5044. **UK**, 1 Supreme Court Rd, Admiralty, **T** 2901 3000. **USA**, 26 Garden Rd, Central, **T** 2523 9011.

Credit card lines
American Express, **T** 2811 6122. **Standard Manhatten Bank**, **T** 2890 8188. **Diners Club**, **T** 2860 1888. **Visa**, **T** 2810 8033. **HSBC**, **T** 2748 4848. **Citibank**, **T** 2823 2323. **MasterCard**, **T** 2598 8038. **Standard Chartered**, **T** 2886 4111.

Cultural institutions
British Council, 3 Supreme Court Rd, Admiralty, **T** 2913 5100, www.britishcouncil.org.hk Predominantly a cultural institute for teaching English, the British Council also organizes events like film festivals, design exhibitions, fashion and visual arts. Also has a library with English newspapers and small internet café, open to non-members. **Alliance Francaise**, 2/F 123 Hennessy Rd, Wan Chai, **T** 2527 7825. French-language library, films, courses and exhibitions. **Goethe Institute**, 14/F Hong Kong Arts Centre, 2 Harbour Rd, Wan Chai, **T** 2802 0088. German-language library, newspapers and video library.

Dentists and doctors
Hotels or chemists will advise of the nearest doctor or dentist. All are English-speaking.

Disabled
While facilities for wheelchairs are not fantastic, the good news is that places are improving and all new constructions like museums and big hotels will have good access. All MTR stations have lifts, as do most of the KCR stations, and the trains are easy to get onto once on the platform. The Government Transport Department has relevant information, www.info.gov.hk

Electricity
The voltage is 220 volts, 50 cycles, and most hotels will provide adapters.

Emergency numbers

Police, Fire and Ambulance, T 999. **Police Crime Hotline**, T 2527 7177. **General Police Inquiries**, T 2860 2000. **Samaritans (Crisis Intervention)** , T 2896 0000.

Hospitals

Queen Mary Hospital, 102 Pokfulam Rd, T 2855 3838. **Queen Elizabeth Hospital**, 30 Gasgoine Rd, Kowloon, T 2958 8888. **Prince of Wales Hospital**, 30-32 Ngan Shing St, Sha Tin, T 2632 2211.

Internet/email

Given how high-tech Hong Kong is, there are surprisingly few internet cafés. The most prominent venues are at **Pacific Coffee**, which has free internet access for their customers in most of their larger branches, with the advantage of having huge sofas to relax on. **Farmer Eo**, 90 Yung Shue Wan Main St, Lamma, and **Bookworm Café**, opposite, have a couple of terminals. **Hippo Bar**, in Mui Wo, Lantau (see p164) has internet access, and there are a few computers bizarrely placed in the middle of Central MTR, LG/F, with free access. **IT Fans**, A & B, G/F & Cockloft Man On Comm Bldg, 12-13 Jubilee St, Central is popular with students.

Language schools

Two places recommended by the HKTB for long- and short-term courses in Mandarin and Cantonese are: **New Asi-Yale-in-China Language Center**, Chinese University of Hong Kong, Fong Shu Chuen Building, Sha Tin, T 2609 6727, www.cuhk.edu.hk/clc/ and **Baptist University Kowloon Tong**, T 3411 5771, www.hkbu.edu.hk

Left luggage

There are left-luggage facilities at the airport.

Libraries

There are many public libraries scattered across the territory but the biggest, newest and best is **Main Central Library**, 66 Causeway Rd, Causeway Bay. *1000-2100, 1300-2100 Wed, 1000-1900 public holidays.* Spread over 12 floors, it has self-charging terminals, an information counter, multi-media information system, renowned for its law reference collection, and has a toy library on 2/F, a play area for kids aged 0-8. Play sessions can be booked on **T** 2921 0386.

Lost property

If left in a taxi, report it to **Taxi Union Lost Report Hotline**, **T** 2385 8288, although they charge $280 to take a report and the emergency service costs $380+. The Union will then contact all the drivers to report articles lost in a taxi. Otherwise, report to the nearest police station, or MTR station if left on the train.

Media

South China Morning Post is the long-established English language daily newspaper with the usual local and foreign news, business and sport, with a lot lifted from English and American papers. They also have a good listings section for entertainment. *Hong Kong Standard* has recently revamped and, although a tabloid, bears little resemblance to gossip-laden rags from back home. *HK Magazine* and *BC Magazine* are both free, weekly listings magazines, although HK is better, and available in cafés and bars especially around Lan Kwai Fong and Wan Chai. Invaluable for entertainment, information and reviews. *Asian Wall Street Journal* and *International Herald Tribune* are, as expected, business-based, and *China Daily* is an English-language paper brought out in China and widely available, giving a great insight into life on the mainland. There is also a good selection of British, Australian and American newspapers and magazines available at major hotels, bookshops and newsstands, especially around Central. The two

English language TV channels are both pretty lousy, the highlight being an American film every night with irritatingly frequent advert breaks. BBC World Service is available 24 hours a day, and the Asian Satellite network Star TV comes out of Hong Kong.

Pharmacies (late night)
Most branches of Watsons and Mannings are open until 2200. Ask at your hotel, or look in *South China Morning Post*.

Police
Hong Kong has one of the world's highest ratios of police to public, which perhaps explains why it is such a safe city. Most of them speak some English, and all the emergency operators at 999 will. Regional offices include: Central, **T** 2522 8882, 2234 9871; Tsim Sha Tsui, **T** 2721 0137, 2730 8194; Sha Tin, **T** 2691 2754, 2601 2176; Lantau South (Mui Wo), **T** 2984 1660, 2984 1408; Cheung Chau, **T** 2981 1217, 2986 9057; Lamma, **T** 2982 0251, 2982 4601; Peng Chau, **T** 2983 0251, 2983 9602.

Post offices
Post is reliable and cheap. Parcels must be sent with appropriate customs forms. Post Restante is available at GPO and Middle Rd branches, collection on production of passport. Some of the offices with parcel service are: **GPO**, 2 Connaught Pl, Central (in front of Star Ferry pier) *0800-1800 Mon-Fri, 0900-1400 Sat.* **Tsim Sha Tsui PO**, G-1/F Hermes House, 10 Middle Rd, Tsim Sha Tsui, *0800-1800 Mon-Fri, 0900-1400 Sat*; **Shop G12**, G/F Elizabeth House, 250-254 Gloucester Rd, Causeway Bay, *0930-1700 Mon-Fri, 0930-1300 Sat.*

Public holidays
Hong Kong enjoys many public holidays, with both Chinese and western festivities bringing many welcome days off. On the following days, banks and other financial institutions will be closed, but most restaurants and shops stay open, apart from

Chinese New Year when many places close down for several days. Museums differ, but should be open on most holidays. Public transport is always available, with different timetables for outlying island ferries. Jan 1, New Year's Day. Mid Jan-mid Feb, 3 days for Chinese New Year. April, Ching Ming Festival, Good Friday and Easter Saturday. May 1, Labour Day. May, Buddha's Birthday. June, Tuen Ng/Dragon Boat Festival. July, 1 HKSAR Establishment Day. Sept, Day following mid-Autumn festival. Oct 1, National Day. Oct, Chung Yeung Festival. Dec 25, Christmas Day. Dec 26, Boxing Day.

Religious services

Hong Kong enjoys much religious tolerance between faiths. In addition to the Chinese temples, there are also over half a million practising Christians who pray in the many Roman Catholic, Protestant and Methodist churches. Details of church services are in the Sunday newspapers. Other places of worship include: **Muslim**: Kowloon Mosque and Islamic Centre, 105 Nathan Rd, Tsim Sha Tsui, **T** 2724 0095; Jamiathe Masjid, 30 Shelley St, Central, **T** 2523 7743. **Jewish**: Ohel Leah Synagogue, 70 Robinson Rd, Mid-Levels, **T** 2857 6095. **Hindu**: Happy Valley Hindu Temple, 1 Wong Nai Chung Rd, Happy Valley; Hindu Mandir, A1/A2 Carnarvon Mansion, 2/F 8-10 Carnarvon Rd, Tsim Sha Tsui. **Sikh**: Khalsa Diwan Sikh Temple, 371 Queen's Rd East, Wan Chai, **T** 2572 4459.

Taxi companies

Hong Kong Island and Kowloon have plenty of taxis and it is rare that you will need to book, but Lantau is unreliable and there are far fewer, so getting to the airport should be planned ahead. (See warning, p29). **Fraternity**, **T** 2527 6324. **Wai Fat**, **T** 2861 1008. **New Territories**, **T** 2457 2266. **Lantau**, **T** 2984 1328.

Telephone

The international code to dial Hong Kong from abroad is +852, and Macau is +853 and there are no area codes for either place. From

Hong Kong to Macau, and vice versa, dial 01 before the number. To call overseas from Hong Kong, the access code is 001. Local calls are free from private phones; public phone boxes charge $1 for around five minutes. Telephone calling cards, making overseas calls cheaper from public phones, are available at Circle K or 7-11 stores starting at $50. There are PCCW (the new name for Hong Kong Telecom) phone boxes in most city areas. **Directory Enquiries**: **T** 1081. **Time and Weather**: **T** 18501. **Collect Calls**: **T** 100010. **Overseas IDD and Cardphone Enquiries**: **T** 10013.

Time
Hong Kong and Macau are in the same time zone as China – 8 hours ahead of GMT.

Toilets
Every shopping centre and department store (of which there are many) has clean toilets, in addition to the numerous hotels, bars, restaurants and fast-food outlets. Most public toilets, for example outside Star Ferry in Central, are surprisingly clean. There are rarely any toilets in MTR stations.

Transport enquiries
City Bus, **T** 2873 0818. **MTR**, **T** 2881 8888. **KCR**, **T** 2602 7799. **New World First Ferry**, **T** 2131 8181. **Hong Kong & Kowloon Ferry**, **T** 2815 6063. **Star Ferry**, **T** 2367 7065. **Hong Kong Macau Hydrofoil**, **T** 2307 0880. **China Travel Service**, **T** 2851 1700. **New Lantao Bus**, **T** 2984 9848. **Peak Tramways**, **T** 2522 0922.

Travel agents
Many agents advertise in the *South China Morning Post*. Beware of those who insist on a non-returnable deposit before they have confirmed your flight. **Air Masters Travel**, **T** 2121 8821, amtravel@netvigator.com **Window Discovery Tours**, **T** 2366 7830/7810, www.mytouragent.com

A sprint through history

c 5000 BC	Formation of Hong Kong's present coastline; first known settlements of fishermen and farmers.
214 BC	Army of the Qin emperor conquered the tribal Yueh people, some of the earliest inhabitants. Hong Kong region became part of the first Chinese Empire with direct rule from Canton.
210 BC	Fall of the Qin dynasty, to independent kingdom by Nan-hai governor.
111 BC	Hong Kong incorporated into Han Empire.
AD 1279	Boy Emperor killed by Mongols, leading to lawlessness and piracy on Lantau.
1513	First contact between Portuguese and Chinese, arrival of Portuguese mariner Jorge Alvares, the first European to sail to the region.
1551	Portuguese settled in Macau and used it as a trading base.
1637	First British ship attempted to sail from Macau to China, but sent back from Canton.
1685	East India Company began trading, coinciding with the rise of colonial power in Asia.
1714	Western traders began sailing to Canton and permitted to land although faced tough restrictions from Chinese rulers.
1773	Decline in trade encouraged British ships to bring opium from India to balance imports of tea, silk and porcelain from China, selling it illegally but with the knowledge of corrupt Chinese officials.

1799	Opium addiction becomes rife forcing Beijing to ban it and driving the trade underground.
1839	Commissioner Lin appointed in Canton to suppress opium trade, ordering surrender of all opium in the hands of foreign merchants. Captain Elliot, British Superintendent of Trade, forced to hand over more than 20,000 chests of opium.
1841	On 25 January, Captain Elliot landed on Hong Kong Island and planted the Union Jack at Possession Point, claiming Hong Kong as a British Colony.
1843	Treaty of Nanking: Britain gained control of Hong Kong Island.
1860	Convention of Peking: Britain gained control of Kowloon and Stonecutters Island.
1898	Convention of Peking: Britain acquired New Territories on 99-year lease. This was followed by some significant population growth and a difficult transition of power. Entrepreneurial property dealers began some major construction on reclaimed land.
1904	Tramline between Kennedy Town and Shau Kei Wan completed.
1910	British section of the Kowloon-Canton Railway completed.
1912	Establishment of Chinese Republic, leading to thousands of refugees from China entering Hong Kong.
1920	Hong Kong flourished as a trading port in inter-war period, especially shipbuilding, ship repairing, manufacturing and textile industries. More land

reclamation around Wan Chai, Sham Shui Po and Lai Chi Kok.

1937	Outbreak of Sino-Japanese War, after Japan seized Manchuria. Hundreds of thousands of Chinese immigrants sought refuge in Hong Kong and camps were set up throughout the territory. Population at the start of Second World War over 1.6 million. Britain became aware of threat from the Japanese.
1939	Plans to defend the territory from the Japanese, including heavy artillery at the south of the island to protect the harbour, and new barracks built at Stanley. Conscription for British subjects introduced and British women and children evacuated.
1941	On 8 December Japan attacked Hong Kong from the north, assisted by the work of a pre-war Japanese intelligence network of waiters, barbers and masseurs working there. Fierce fighting led to British Army surrendering Hong Kong to the Japanese on 25 December.
1942	Prisoners-of-war held at Sham Shui Po Barracks;, overcrowding later relieved when 3,000 men were sent to Japan as labourers and Chinese were urged to return to the mainland.
1945	Japan surrendered on 14 August and ships from the British Pacific Fleet arrived to end occupation. Chinese civilians returned at around 100,000 per month, escaping the new Chinese communist regime. Population rose from 600,000 to 1.8 million by end of 1947.
1946	Outbreak of Chinese Civil War closed the border with Hong Kong causing downturn in economy.

1947	Formation of new government departments to deal with rapid population growth. Influx of refugees, especially from Shanghai, provided workforce to help create Hong Kong's post-war growth. Tax policies attracted foreign investment.
1953	On 25 December, a huge fire at squatter huts at Shek Kip Mei caused homelessness for 50,000 people, and forced the Government to start radical programme of rehousing and slum clearance.
1963	Exports recovered, exceeding their 1951 level, and manufacturing industries thrived especially in textiles, plastics, electronics and watches.
1967	Communist-inspired riots broke out, pro-Peking demonstrations were held outside Government House, causing slowdown in economy. Government took emergency action to preserve law and order to diffuse the tension.
1972	End of Vietnam War and Sir Murray MacLehose, Hong Kong's new governor succeeded in tackling corruption and immigration over the next decade. China cultivated closer economic and diplomatic ties with the West.
1973	Plans for three 'first generation' towns: Tsuen Wan, Sha Tin and Tuen Mun.
1974	Influx of thousands of refugees from Vietnam.
1984	Joint Declaration signed by Britain and China, agreeing sovereignty of Hong Kong would revert back to China in 1997.
1989	Tiananmen Square massacre brought nearly a million protestors out in Hong Kong, and genuine

worry of the state of democracy after handover to China in 1997. Over 50,000 Vietnamese Boat People arrive in Hong Kong.

1997   1 July Hong Kong becomes a Special Administrative Region of People's Republic of China, under a 'one country, two systems' form of rule, with Tung Chee-hwa as the Chief Executive. Start of the Asian financial crisis, collapse in Hong Kong's economy and tourism.

1998   Official recession, with record unemployment.

2000   Beijing tried to prevent Hong Kong press from reporting Taiwanese pro-independence movement, and outlawed and persecuted Falun Gong followers, both causing fears of democratic freedom in Hong Kong.

2003   SARS virus causes panic and has a huge impact on tourism and creating more problems for a poor economy.

Sep 2003   Announcement that Article 23, the section of the Basic Law and mini constitution relating to subversion, treason and secession (see p15) and the most worrying post-97 threat to free speech, has been indefinitely shelved following an unprecedented protest on Hong Kong's streets.

Books

Fiction

Clavell, J, *Noble House: A Novel of Contemporary Hong Kong*. (1981), Flame Hodder. Set in Hong Kong in 1963, the action spans a little over a week and is packed with high adventure from kidnapping, murder, financial double-dealing, fires, floods and landslides. Just another week in the life of the Russian, Chinese and British businessmen who manoeuvre and manipulate for the control of Hong Kong's oldest trading house under the eyes of the KGB, CIA and PRC, with corporate skulduggery in abundance.

Clavell, J, *Tai-Pan*. (1966), Flame Hodder. Another volume in his popular Asia series, inspired by his stay in the territory in the 60s, this focuses on Hong Kong and its most powerful trading company. The tale unfolds of Dirk Straun, a pirate, smuggler and ruthless individual who finds glory beyond his wildest dreams as the Tai-Pan, or supreme leader, of Hong Kong.

Lanchester, J, *Fragrant Harbor*. (2002), Faber and Faber. This combination of two excellent novels presents a colonial narrative beginning in the 1930s, within a complex tale of big business at the turn of the 21st century. The hero, Tom Stewart, from England travels to Hong Kong in 1935 as it embarks on its prosperous years, and on his voyage out he is made the object of a bizarre bet between a Chinese nun and an anti-Catholic English businessman. It portrays colonial life in the 1930s, the Japanese occupation during the Second World War, the post-war boom, Triads and the handover.

Theroux, P, *Kowloon Tong: A Novel of Hong Kong*. (1998) Penguin. Neville "Bunt" Mullard and his awful mum Betty, bigoted and quintessentially English, dread the end of colonial rule and therefore the end of 50 glorious years of running the family textile factory. Insulated against Chinese culture for so long, they are forced to deal with the dodgy Mr Hung who wants to buy the business and will use ugly tactics if necessary, much to the disgust of the insipid Bunt.

Non-fiction

Bordwell, D, *Planet Hong Kong*. (2000), Harvard University Press. A self-confessed fanatic of Hong Kong films, Bordwell tries to explain and understand the relationship between art and entertainment in popular cinema. He gives an introduction to the genre, and explanation of the industry's background, production practices and film structure and style.

Cheung, J and **Teoh**, A, *Hong Kong - A Guide to Recent Architecture*. (1998), Ellipsis. A gem of a book, albeit tiny, with architectural information and design history of many buildings in Hong Kong giving a great insight into the workings of the city and its aesthetic development. With more of a slant on contemporary structures, it includes everything from shopping centres, restaurants to cultural centres – and even illegal façades.

Dannen, F and **Long**, B, *Hong Kong Babylon - An Insider's Guide to the Hollywood of the East*. (1997), Faber and Faber. A broad overview of contemporary Hong Kong cinema and what it offers the western world, with selected interviews with film-makers, filmographies and plot summaries of movies from New Wave to present day. It also gives an interesting list of the top 30 Hong Kong films, as selected by 12 critics (including *Bullet in the Head*; *Center Stage* and *Chungking Express*).

Moss, P, *Skylines Hong Kong* (2000), FormAsia. A beautiful large-format book, heavy on colour photographs which details individual buildings, not all of them obvious. From old colonial relics like the Hong Kong Club, to modern shopping centres like Taikoo Place, it gives the history and architectural detail and makes a great souvenir.

Patten, C, *East and West*. (1999), Pan. Written by Hong Kong's last British Governor on the power, freedom and future of the territory. This draws on his experiences during his five years at the helm. Having seen China at its very worst and also in a more positive light, he develops arguments about Asia, the conduct of economic policy, and the relationship between political freedom and economic liberty. Patten also analyses the developing relationship between China and the west, which he witnessed during such a crucial era.

Roberts, JAG, *China to Chinatown – Chinese Food in the West*. (2002), Globalities. Essential for food lovers and especially those who wonder how there has come to be a Chinese takeaway or restaurant on every high street in Britain and America. A good introduction to the history of the food, and how the west discovered it through Marco Polo, through the western perception of Chinese food during the 20th century until the globalization of the cuisine.

Schechter, D, *Falun Gong's Challenge to China - Spiritual Practice or Evil Cult?* (2001), Akaskic Books. The US journalist presents a detailed account of the controversial spiritual practice, which revolves around peaceful meditation and philosophy, that in nine years rocketed from the backwaters of China onto the front pages of international newspapers. It analyses why it has proved to be so threatening to China's old guard, and how it has gained support around the world.

Snow, P, *The Fall of Hong Kong: Britain, China and the Japanese Occupation*. (2003), Yale University Press. This heavy tome is a historical account of the Japanese occupation from the viewpoint of the Hong Kong Chinese, the British, Japanese and Mainland Chinese. It reveals the widespread desertion of the British by the Chinese personnel during the invasion and the cruelty of the Japanese to the Chinese.

South China Morning Post, *Hong Kong Hikes*. (2002), SCMP. Highly recommended for anyone wanting to hike around the outlying regions of Hong Kong, this user-friendly collection has 20 of the best walks, all on individual cards on a ring binder, designed to be pulled out and placed in its own plastic wallet. Each one contains good descriptions, details and practical information for walks around Lantau, New Territories and Hong Kong Island.

Wiltshire, T, *Old Kong Kong*. (2003), FormAsia. A beautiful, boxed collection of three books looking at the history of Hong Kong between 1860 to 1997 through black and white photographs. Starting with the early years of the imperial island, moving on to scenes of crowded streets, swinging pigtails and starched, white collars, through to Hong Kong's most dramatic half-century ending with the signing of the Joint Declaration and the midnight Handover Ceremony.

Index

Credits

Footprint credits

Editor: Sarah Thorowgood
Map editor: Sarah Sorensen

Publisher: Patrick Dawson
Series developed by Rachel Fielding
Cartography: Robert Lunn, Claire
Benison, Kevin Feeney, Shane Feeney
Proof-reading: Claire Boobbyer
Design: Mytton Williams

Photography credits

Front cover: Emma Levine (chopsticks)
Inside: Emma Levine (p1 Big Buddha
Lantau, p5 Lantau Temple, p35 Chi Lin
Nunnery, p85 Tai O fish)
Generic images: John Matchett
Back cover: Alamy (dragon dance)

Print

Manufactured in Italy by LegoPrint.
Pulp from sustainable forests.

Footprint feedback

We try as hard as we can to make
each Footprint guide as up to date as
possible but, of course, things always
change. If you want to let us know
about your experiences – good, bad
or ugly – then don't delay, go to
www.footprintbooks.com and send
in your comments.

Publishing information

Footprint Hong Kong
1st edition
Text and maps © Footprint
Handbooks Ltd November 2003

ISBN 1 903471 82 6
CIP DATA: a catalogue record for this
book is available from the British Library

Published by Footprint
6 Riverside Court
Lower Bristol Road
Bath, BA2 3DZ, UK
T +44 (0)1225 469141
F +44 (0)1225 469461
discover@footprintbooks.com
www.footprintbooks.com

Distributed in the USA by
Publishers Group West

Complete title list

Latin America & Caribbean

Argentina
Barbados (P)
Bolivia
Brazil
Caribbean Islands
Central America & Mexico
Chile
Colombia
Costa Rica
Cuba
Cusco & the Inca Trail
Dominican Republic
Ecuador & Galápagos
Guatemala
Havana (P)
Mexico
Nicaragua
Peru
Rio de Janeiro
South American Handbook
Venezuela

North America

Vancouver (P)
Western Canada

Africa

Cape Town (P)
East Africa
Libya
Marrakech &
  the High Atlas
Marrakech (P)
Morocco
Namibia
South Africa
Tunisia
Uganda

Middle East

Egypt
Israel
Jordan
Syria & Lebanon

Asia

Bali
Bangkok & the Beaches
Cambodia
Goa
Hong King (P)
India
Indian Himalaya
Indonesia
Laos
Malaysia
Nepal
Pakistan
Rajasthan & Gujarat
Singapore
South India
Sri Lanka
Sumatra
Thailand
Tibet
Vietnam

Australasia

Australia
East Coast Asutralia
New Zealand
Sydney (P)
West Coast Australia

Europe

Andalucía
Barcelona
Berlin (P)
Bilbao (P)
Bologna (P)
Copenhagen (P)
Croatia
Dublin (P)
Edinburgh (P)
England
Glasgow
Ireland
Lisbon (P)
London
Madrid (P)
Naples (P)
Northern Spain
Paris (P)
Reykjavik (P)
Scotland
Seville (P)
Scotland Highlands
  & Islands
Spain
Turin (P)
Turkey
Verona (P)

(P) denotes pocket
Handbook

For a different view…
choose a Footprint

Over 100 Footprint travel guides
Covering more than 150 of the world's most exciting countries and cities in Latin America, the Caribbean, Africa, the Indian sub-continent, Australasia, North America, Southeast Asia, the Middle East and Europe.

Discover so much more…
The finest writers. In-depth knowledge. Entertaining and accessible. Critical restaurant and hotels reviews. Lively descriptions of all the attractions. Get away from the crowds.

What the papers say...

"I carried the South American Handbook from Cape Horn to Cartagena and consulted it every night for two and a half months. I wouldn't do that for anything else except my hip flask."
Michael Palin, BBC Full Circle

"My favourite series is the Handbook series published by Footprint and I especially recommend the Mexico, Central and South America Handbooks."
Boston Globe

"If 'the essence of real travel' is what you have been secretly yearning for all these years, then Footprint are the guides for you."
Under 26 magazine

"Who should pack Footprint–readers who want to escape the crowd."
The Observer

"Footprint can be depended on for accurate travel information and for imparting a deep sense of respect for the lands and people they cover."
World News

"The guides for intelligent, independently-minded souls of any age or budget."
Indie Traveller

Mail order
Available worldwide in bookshops and on-line. Footprint travel guides can also be ordered directly from us in Bath, via our website www.footprintbooks.com or from the address on the credits page of this book.

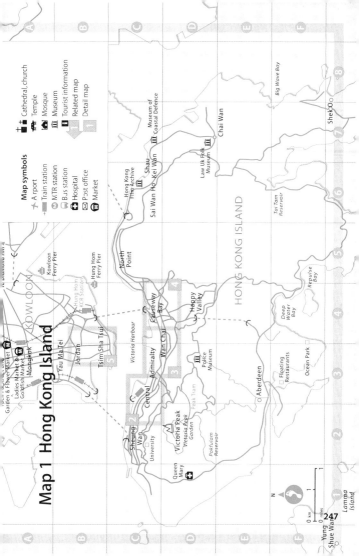

Map 1 Hong Kong Island

Map symbols

- ✈ A rport
- 🚉 Train station
- Ⓜ M:TR station
- 🚌 B.s station
- ✚ Hospital
- ✉ Post office
- 🏪 Market
- ✝ Cathedral, church
- 卍 Temple
- ☪ Mosque
- 🏛 Museum
- 🛈 Tourist information
- Related map
- Detail map

Garden & Flower Market

Ladies Market & Goldfish Market

Mongkok

KOWLOON

Kowloon Ferry Pier

Hung Hom (KCR Station)

Hung Hom Ferry Pier

Yau Ma Tei

Jordan

Tsim Sha Tsui

Victoria Harbour

North Point

Hong Kong Film Archive

Museum of Coastal Defence 🏛

Shau Sai Wan Ho Kei Wan

Chai Wan

Law Uk Folk Museum 🏛

Shek O

Big Wave Bay

Sheung Wan

University

Central

Admiralty

Wan Chai

Causeway Bay

Happy Valley

Police Museum 🏛

HONG KONG ISLAND

Tai Tam Reservoir

Victoria Peak

Victoria Peak Garden

Peak Tram

Aberdeen

Floating Restaurants

Ocean Park

Repulse Bay

Deep Water Bay

Queen Mary ✚

Pokfulam Reservoir

N

0 km
0 miles

Yung Shue Wan

Lamma Island

247

Map 2 Sheung Wan & Central

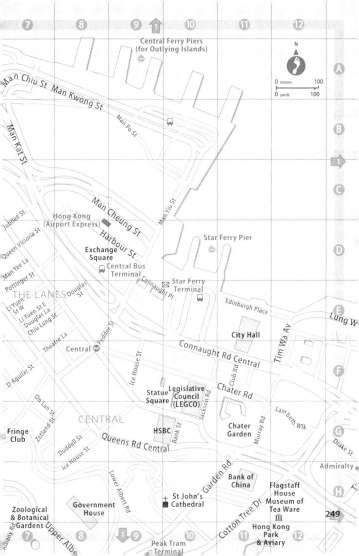

Central Ferry Piers
(for Outlying Islands)

N

| 0 metres | 100 |
| 0 yards | 100 |

Man Chiu St Man Kwong St

Man Kat St

Man Po St

Man Cheung St

Man Yiu St

Hong Kong
(Airport Express)

Harbour St

Star Ferry Pier

**Exchange
Square**

Central Bus
Terminal

Connaught Pl

Star Ferry
Terminal

Jubilee St

Queen Victoria St

Man Yee La

Pottinger St

Li Yuen St E

THE LANES

Li Yuen St W

Douglas St

Douglas La

Chiu Lung St

Theatre La

Pedder St

Ice House St

Central Ⓜ

Edinburgh Place

City Hall

Connaught Rd Central

Club Rd

Chater Rd

Tim Wa Av

Lung W

D'Aguilar St

On Lan St

Zetland St

CENTRAL

Statue
Square

**Legislative
Council
(LEGCO)**

Jackson Rd

Bank St

**Chater
Garden**

Murray Rd

Lambeth Wlk

Drake St

Admiralty

**Fringe
Club**

Duddell St

Ice House St

HSBC

Queens Rd Central

Lower Albert Rd

Garden Rd

✝ **St John's
Cathedral**

**Bank of
China**

**Flagstaff
House
Museum of
Tea Ware**
🏛

**Zoological
& Botanical
Gardens**

Albany Rd

**Government
House**

Upper Albe

Cotton Tree Dr

**Hong Kong
Park & Aviary**

Peak Tram
Terminal

249

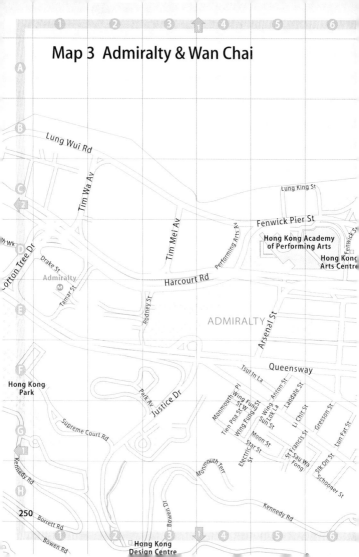

Map 3 Admiralty & Wan Chai

Lung Wui Rd

Tim Wa Av

Tim Mei Av

Performing Arts Av

Lung King St

Fenwick Pier St

Fenwick St

Hong Kong Academy
of Performing Arts

Hong Kong
Arts Centre

'th Wk

Cotton Tree Dr

Drake St

Admiralty

Ⓜ

Tamar St

Harcourt Rd

Rodney St

ADMIRALTY

Arsenal St

Queensway

Tsui In La

Hong Kong
Park

Park Av

Justice Dr

Monmouth Pl

Wing Fung St

Tien Poa St W

Wing Fung St

Anton St

Sun Lok La

Landale St

Li Chit St

Gresson St

Lun Fat St

Supreme Court Rd

Moon St

St Francis St

Kennedy Rd

Moon St

Star St

Electric St

St Sau Wa Pong

Sik On St

Schooner St

Monmouth Terr

Bowen Dr

Kennedy Rd

250

Borrett Rd

Bowen Rd

Hong Kong
Design Centre

② ③ ⬇④ ⑤ ⑥

Swimming
Pool

Lau Li St

Hing Fat St

Tsing Fling St

Ngan Mok St

Yacht St

Lau Sin St

Victoria Park

Ⓜ Tin Hau

Dragon Terr

Dragon Rd

New Eastern Terr

Yee King Rd

Causeway Rd

CAUSEWAY BAY

Gloucester Rd

Sugar St

ee Wo St

Irving St

eswick
St

Leighton Rd

Moreton Terr

Tung Lo Wan Dr

Tun Lo Wan Rd

Tun Lo Wan Rd

School St

King St

Ormsby St

Lay Yin St

Jones St

Warren St

Shepherd St

Sun Chun St

Wun Sha St

Lai Tak Tsuen Rd

Haven St

Ka Ning Path

Cotton Path

Tai Hang Rd

Yik Kwan Av

LI Kwan Av

Fuk Kwan Av

Eastern Hospital Road

Wang Fung Terr

Tai Hang Rd

**South China
Athletic Stadium**

Tai Hang Dri

King's R

N

0 metres 100
0 yards 100

Ⓐ
Ⓑ
Ⓒ
Ⓓ
Ⓔ
Ⓕ
Ⓖ
Ⓗ

7 8 9 10 11 12

253

ium Path

Tai Hang

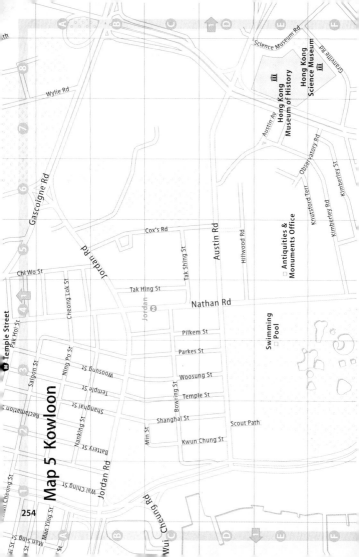

Map 5 Kowloon

254

M Temple Street

Science Museum Rd

Granville Rd

Hong Kong Science Museum

Hong Kong Museum of History

Austin Av

Wylie Rd

Observatory Rd

Knutsford Terr

Kimberley St

Kimberley Rd

Gascoigne Rd

Cox's Rd

Austin Rd

Jordan Rd

Tak Shing St

Hillwood Rd

Chi Wo St

Pak Hoi St

Cheong Lok St

Tak Hing St

Nathan Rd

Jordan

Antiquities & Monuments Office

Pilkem St

Parkes St

Swimming Pool

Saigon St

Ning Po St

Woosung St

Woosung St

Bowring St

Temple St

Temple St

Shanghai St

Shanghai St

Nanking St

Reclamation St

Battery St

Min St

Kwun Chung St

Scout Path

Wai Ching St

Jordan Rd

Man Ying St

Wui Cheung Rd

Man Ying St

Mody Rd

Mody Sq

Salisbury Rd

Chatham Rd South

Granville

Hau Fook St.

Cameron Rd

Prat Av

Minden Av

Granville Av

Carnarvon Rd

Hart Av

Hanoi Rd

Cameron La

Humphrey's Av

Cornwall Av   Minden Row

Bristol Av

Mody Rd

Middle Rd

Chungking Mansions

⊠

Peninsula Hotel

Hong Kong Space Museum
🏛

Hong Kong Museum of Art
🏛

Parklane Boulevard

Kowloon Mosque & Islamic Centre
☪

Nathan Rd (Golden Mile)

Salisbury Rd

Kowloon Park

Tsim Sha Tsui

Lock Rd

TSIM SHA TSUI

Hankow Rd

Halphong Rd

Chang St

Ashley Rd

Kowloon Park Dr

Peking Rd

Hong Kong Cultural Centre

Cultural Centre Plaza

Canton Rd

Tsim Sha Tsui Star Ferry Terminal

Star Ferry Pier

Gateway Boulevard

Ocean Terminal

China Ferry Terminal

N

0 metres   100
0 yards   100

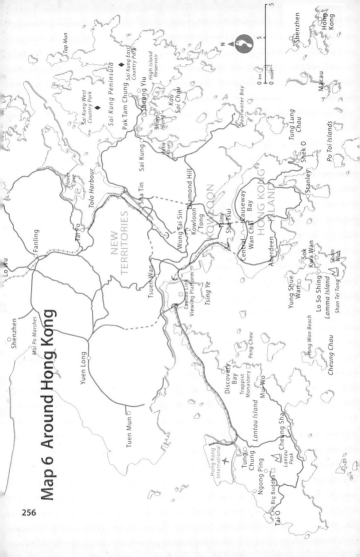

Map 6 Around Hong Kong